Praise for Thich Nhat Hanh and *The Sun My Heart*

"The monk who taught the world mindfulness."

— *TIME*

"Thich Nhat Hanh shows us the connection between personal inner peace and peace on earth."

— HIS HOLINESS THE DALAI LAMA

"Thich Nhat Hanh is a holy man, for he is humble and devout. He is a scholar of immense intellectual capacity. His ideas for peace, if applied, would build a monument to ecumenism, to world brotherhood, to humanity."

— DR. MARTIN LUTHER KING, JR.

"*The Sun My Heart* first came into my hands over three decades ago, and it is still my most cherished book by Thich Nhat Hanh. Ever again it brings the freshness of morning, a luminous, clear-eyed sanity at the core of the Dharma. Here is born the courage to embrace our suffering world, which has grounded and guided me through the years."

— JOANNA MACY, AUTHOR OF *A WILD LOVE FOR THE WORLD: JOANNA MACY AND THE WORK OF OUR TIME*

"Thich Nhat Hanh's work, on and off the page, has proven to be the antidote to our modern pain and sorrows. Here is a monumental, life-giving mind, preserved as textual force. And that's what I feel reading and practicing his teachings: that I am being acted on by a compassion equal to and pervasive as gravity itself. His books help me be more human, more *me* than I was before."

—OCEAN VUONG, AUTHOR OF
ON EARTH WE'RE BRIEFLY GORGEOUS

"Thich Nhat Hanh is a great teacher. I have studied him, his work, his passage through life, with gratitude and joy. Through his writings, his public offerings, his insights, I've gained vision and clarity; I've often felt it would be impossible to find a more lucid, determined, and courageous soul."

—ALICE WALKER, AUTHOR OF *THE COLOR PURPLE*

"Thich Nhat Hanh is among the most revered leaders in the world. His teachings and mindfulness practices have deeply influenced my journey through life. He is a torch of wisdom lighting the path ahead, generating the compassion, love, and understanding we need to create peace for ourselves and the world."

—MARC BENIOFF, CHAIR AND CEO, SALESFORCE

"Thich Nhat Hanh does not merely teach peace; Thich Nhat Hanh *is* peace."

—ELIZABETH GILBERT, AUTHOR OF *EAT, PRAY, LOVE*

"Thich Nhat Hanh's words are like water. Simple, pure, transparent, and absolutely indispensable for life."

—ALEJANDRO GONZÁLEZ IÑÁRRITU, DIRECTOR
OF *BIRDMAN* AND *THE REVENANT*

"How is it that a Vietnamese Buddhist monk who teaches mindfulness could inspire Martin Luther King and become one of the great nonviolent activists of the twenty-first century? Like no other teacher, Thich Nhat Hanh shows us the revolutionary possibilities of building social movements based on compassion, for both ourselves and others."

— PROFESSOR JOHN A. POWELL, DIRECTOR OF THE OTHERING & BELONGING INSTITUTE AT UC BERKELEY

"I first met Thich Nhat Hanh in 1968 in Paris. That was the time of rising counterculture, protest against the Vietnam War and student uprising. At that time his presence in Paris was like a soothing rain in dry heat. Ever since, for more than fifty years, he has been the conscience of humanity. He has been a compassionate catalyst of spiritual awakening, social harmony, and ecological awareness. He has nurtured the human spirit with dedication, determination, and delight. He is humble and gentle yet powerfully persuasive and strong-willed. It has been a joy of my life to know him and follow his teachings."

— SATISH KUMAR, EDITOR EMERITUS OF *RESURGENCE & ECOLOGIST* MAGAZINE AND FOUNDER OF SCHUMACHER COLLEGE

The Sun
My Heart

Also by Thich Nhat Hanh

Anger

The Art of Communicating

The Art of Living

The Art of Power

At Home in the World

Awakening of the Heart

Be Free Where You Are

Being Peace

Breathe, You Are Alive!

Call Me by My True Names

Chanting from the Heart

Creating True Peace

The Diamond That Cuts through Illusion

Fear

Fragrant Palm Leaves

The Heart of the Buddha's Teaching

Hermitage among the Clouds

How to Love

Joyfully Together

Living Buddha, Living Christ

Love in Action

Love Letter to the Earth

Master Tang Hoi

The Miracle of Mindfulness

No Death, No Fear

No Mud, No Lotus

Old Path White Clouds

Peace Is Every Step

Present Moment Wonderful Moment

The Raft Is Not the Shore

Reconciliation

Transformation and Healing

Understanding Our Mind

The World We Have

The Sun My Heart

Reflections on Mindfulness,
Concentration, and Insight

Thich Nhat Hanh

Foreword by Christiana Figueres

PARALLAX PRESS
BERKELEY, CALIFORNIA

PARALLAX PRESS
PO BOX 7355
BERKELEY, CALIFORNIA 94707
WWW.PARALLAX.ORG

Parallax Press is the publishing division of the Plum Village
Community of Engaged Buddhism, Inc.

Translated from the Vietnamese by Anh-Huong
Nguyen, Elin Sand, and Annabel Laity

Thanks to Tyrone Cashman, Roger Jones,
Brit Pyland, Sara Norwood, and Tom Ginsberg

Cover and text design by Katie Eberle
Composition by Happenstance Type-O-Rama
Cover art by Atelier Atelier

ISBN: 978-1-946764-70-6
LCCN: 2020029160

3 4 5 / 23 22 21

Contents

Foreword

I FIRST CAME ACROSS Thich Nhat Hanh's teachings in 2013, when I was leading the international climate change negotiations and was suddenly dropped into the deepest personal crisis I have ever had. I found myself standing on the sharp abyss of emotional agony, and yet was conscious of the fact that I could not abdicate my responsibility of holding the global reins of what eventually became the 2015 Paris Agreement on Climate Change. My heart had shrivelled to nothingness, but my head had to vehemently push forward to converge the efforts of 195 governments and thousands of stakeholders representing the global economy into one ambitious legal agreement.

Universal causes and conditions aligned to get me to the European Institute of Applied Buddhism in Germany, which I had never even heard of before. That is where I started my study of Thay's teachings. Slowly but surely, I began to understand the deep art of transforming pain into learning, and eventually into gratitude and grace. "No mud, no lotus." Not an easy journey, but the one that liberates us. I later started to frequent the beautiful Plum Village, Thay's main monastery in southwest France. Several Brothers and Sisters lovingly took me under their wing, sharing Dharma light in moments of despair and darkness. Today I continue to walk in Thay's footsteps, witnessing, in his words, how "The tears that I shed yesterday have become rain," upon my own inner soil and how they are watering my seeds of love, compassion, and peace.

It has always been important to water the seeds of love and peace, but perhaps now with ever more intensified purpose. We find ourselves at a historically unprecedented convergence of global crises. The chronic climate change crisis, the biodiversity crisis, and the inequality crisis have all been lingering at our doorstep for decades. And now they have all converged upon each other, exacerbating their potential destructive impact on all living beings. However, the convergence of the crises is at the same time an opportunity for us to see beyond the evident obstacles in order to converge our deeper understanding of the way forward.

Thay's timeless handwritten book *The Sun My Heart* is being republished in 2020, a year unquestionably unique in human history. It was intended to be the year in which critical steps on climate change and biodiversity would be taken. Instead, the COVID-19 pandemic has swept across the world, forcing the Great Pause. The world has stopped its pounding busyness and millions have been confined to their homes for months. Home, work, and school have lost their rhythm, and travel has lost its meaning. All manner of forms and structures have been lifted, suspended in a timeless unknown of uncertain evolution.

We are in a fertile suspension that already contains the seeds of everything that will become. While it seems that the "outside world" has paused, it is actually only the constant compulsion to rush forward that is suspended, opening bountiful space and time for deeper wakefulness. It is precisely in this fecundity of potential that Thay's writings bid us to peaceful and heart-filled presence. As many of our "sense windows" are closed, it is a fortuitous moment for us to pause our mental compulsions and look attentively "inside," exploring the bounty of our mindful awareness.

As when originally published, so now again, *The Sun My Heart* beckons us into the understanding of the deep interconnections among all living beings, into the immutable reality of all living forms interbeing and interflowing with and through each other. Taking us tenderly by the hand, Thay invites us to breathe into the nonduality of our "inside" and "outside" world, to the realization that there is neither "inner" nor "outer." We are endlessly interwoven with every ray of sun, every drop of rain, every speck of dust, every leaf, and every flower. We rely on one another for existence. That is why we can and must care for every cloud, every tree, and every river as we care for ourselves. And that is why we have limitless possibilities for co-creating a better world. That realization is home.

I write these few words as I sit at home, watching the Pacific Ocean lovingly lapping onto the nearby shore. Over my shoulder, I hear Thay whispering, "The wave lives the life of a wave, and at the same time, the life of water. When you breathe, you breathe for all of us."

CHRISTIANA FIGUERES

JULY 2020

Introduction

MEDITATORS SINCE THE BEGINNING OF time have known that they must use their own eyes and the language of their own times to express their insight. Wisdom is a living stream, not an icon to be preserved in a museum. Only when a practitioner finds the spring of wisdom in his or her own life can it flow to future generations. Keeping the torch of wisdom glowing is the work of all of us who know how to clear a path through the forest in order to walk on ahead.

Our insight and our language are inseparable from the times in which we live. For many years now, the East has followed the West down the path of technological and material development, to the point of neglecting its own spiritual values. In our world, technology is the main force behind economics and politics, but those in the forefront of science have begun to see something similar to what the spiritual disciplines of the East discovered long ago. If we can survive our times, the gap that separates science and spirituality will close, and East and West will meet one another on the path to discover true mind. Those in whom the seeds of this important endeavor have already been sown can start working toward that convergence right now, using their own daily mindful lives.

This small book was not written to show off any special knowledge of the author. (In fact, there is not much for him to show off.) It prefers to be a friend rather than a book. You can take it with you on the bus or subway, just as you do your coat or your scarf. It can give you small moments of joy at any time. You may like to read a few lines, then close it and put it back in your pocket, and read another few lines sometime later. If you find a paragraph that is difficult or complicated, just skip over it and try the next one. You can return to it later and maybe you will find that it is not so complicated after all. Chapter Five, which is the last one, is quite pleasant to read. You can start there if you like.

Please draw on your own experience to understand this book. Do not be intimidated by any of the words or ideas. Only as the author of the text yourself will you find the joy and the strength necessary to journey from mindfulness to insight.

NHAT HANH
JANUARY 1988

Sunshine and Green Leaves

Thanh Thuy's Apple Juice

TODAY THREE CHILDREN, two girls and a little boy, came from the village to play with Thanh Thuy (pronounced "Tahn Tui"). The four of them ran off to play on the hillside behind our house and were gone for about an hour when they returned to ask for something to drink. I took the last bottle of homemade apple juice and gave them each a full glass, serving Thuy last. Since her juice was from the bottom of the bottle, it had some pulp in it. When she noticed the particles, she pouted and refused to drink it. So the four children went back to their games on the hillside, and Thuy had not drunk anything.

Half an hour later, while I was meditating in my room, I heard her calling. Thuy wanted to get herself a glass of cold water, but even on tiptoes she couldn't reach the faucet. I reminded her of the glass of juice on the table and asked her to drink that first. Turning to look at it, she saw that the pulp had settled and the juice looked clear and delicious.

She went to the table and took the glass with both hands. After drinking half of it, she put it down and asked, "Is this a different glass, Uncle Monk?" (a common term for Vietnamese children to use when addressing an older monk).

"No," I answered. "It's the same one as before. It sat quietly for a bit, and now it's clear and delicious." Thuy looked at the glass again. "It really is good. Was it meditating like you, Uncle Monk?" I laughed and patted her head. "Let's say that I imitate the apple juice when I sit; that is closer to the truth."

Every night at Thuy's bedtime, I sit in meditation. I let her sleep in the same room, near where I am sitting. We have agreed that while I am sitting, she will go to bed without talking. In that peaceful atmosphere, rest comes easily to her, and she is usually asleep within five or ten minutes. When I finish sitting, I cover her with a blanket.

Thanh Thuy is the child of "boat people." She is not yet four and a half years old. She crossed the seas with her father and arrived in Malaysia in April of last year. Her mother stayed in Vietnam. When her father arrived here in France, he left Thuy with us for several months while he went to Paris to look for a job. I taught her the Vietnamese alphabet and some popular folk songs from our country. She is very intelligent, and after two weeks she was able to spell out and slowly read "Ivan the Fool" by Leo Tolstoy, which I translated into Vietnamese from the French.

Every night Thanh Thuy sees me sit. I told her that I am "sitting in meditation" without explaining what it means or why I do it. Every night when she sees me wash my face, put on my robes, and light a stick of incense to make the room fragrant, she knows that soon I will begin "meditating." She also knows that it is time for her to brush her teeth, change into pajamas, and go quietly to bed. I have never had to remind her.

Without a doubt, Thuy thought that the apple juice was sitting for a while to clear itself, just like her Uncle Monk. "Was it meditating like you?" I think that Thanh Thuy, not yet four and a half, understands the meaning of meditation without any explanation. The apple juice became clear after resting awhile. In the same way, if we rest in meditation awhile, we too become clear. This clarity refreshes us and gives us strength and serenity. As we feel ourselves refreshed, our surroundings also become refreshed. Children like to be near us, not just to get candy and hear stories. They like to be near us because they can feel this freshness.

Tonight a guest has come. I fill a glass with the last of the apple juice and put it on the table in the middle of the meditation room. Thuy is already fast asleep, and I invite my friend to sit very quietly, just like the apple juice.

A River of Perceptions

We sit for about forty minutes. I notice my friend smiling as he looks at the juice. It has become very clear. "And you, my friend, are you clear? Even if you have not settled as thoroughly as the apple juice, don't you feel a little less agitated, less fidgety, and less disturbed? The smile on your lips hasn't faded yet, but I think you doubt that you might become as clear as the apple juice, even if we continue to sit for hours.

"The glass of juice has a very stable base. But you, your sitting is not so sure. Those tiny bits of pulp only have to follow the laws of nature to fall gently to the bottom of the glass. But your thoughts obey no such law. To the contrary, they buzz feverishly, like a swarm of bees, and so you think you cannot settle like the apple juice.

"You tell me that people, living beings with the capacity to think and to feel, cannot be compared with a glass of juice. I agree, but I also know that we can do what the apple juice does, and more. We can be at peace, not only while sitting, but also while walking and working.

"Perhaps you don't believe me, because forty minutes have passed and you tried so hard but weren't able to achieve the peace you hoped for. Thuy is sleeping peacefully, her breathing is light. Why don't we light another candle before continuing our conversation?

"Little Thuy sleeps this way effortlessly. You know those nights when sleep eludes you, and the harder you try to sleep the less you can? You are trying to force yourself to be peaceful, and you feel the resistance inside of you. This same sort of resistance is felt by many people during their first experiences with meditation. The more they try to calm themselves, the more restless they become. The Vietnamese think this is because they are victims of demons or bad karma, but really this resistance is born out of our very efforts to be peaceful. The effort itself becomes oppressive. Our thoughts and feelings flow like a river. If we try to stop the flow of a river, we will meet the resistance of the water. It is better to flow with it, and then we may be able to guide it in ways we want it to go. We must not attempt to halt it.

"Keep in mind that the river must flow and that we are going to follow it. We must be aware of every little stream that joins it. We must be aware of all the thoughts, feelings, and sensations that arise in us—of their birth, duration, and disappearance. Do you see? Now the resistance begins to disappear. The river of perceptions is still flowing, but no longer in darkness. It is now flowing in the sunlight of awareness. To keep this sun always shining inside of us, illuminating each rivulet, each pebble, each bend in the river, is the practice of meditation. To practice meditation is, first of all, to observe and to follow these details.

"At the moment of awareness we feel we are in control, even though the river is still there, still flowing. We feel ourselves at peace, but this isn't the 'peace' of the apple juice. Being at peace doesn't mean our thoughts and feelings are frozen. Being at peace is not the same as being anesthetized. A peaceful mind does not mean a mind empty of thoughts, sensations, and emotions. A peaceful mind is not an absent one. It is clear that thoughts and feelings alone do not comprise the whole of our being. Fury, hatred, shame, faith, doubt, impatience, disgust, desire, sorrow, and anguish are also mind. Hope, inhibition, intuition, instinct, subconscious, and unconscious minds are equally part of the self. Vijñanavada Buddhism discusses at length the eight principal and fifty-one subordinate mental conditions. If you have the time, you may want to look at these writings. They embrace all psychological phenomena."[1]

Sunshine and Green Leaves

Beginning meditators usually think they must suppress all thoughts and feelings (often called "false mind") in order to create conditions favorable to concentration and understanding (called "true mind"). They use methods such as focusing their attention on an object or counting their breaths to try to block out thoughts and feelings. Concentrating on an object and counting the breath are excellent methods, but they should not be used for suppression or repression. We know that as soon as there is repression, there is rebellion; repression entails rebellion. True mind and false mind are one. Denying one is denying the other. Suppressing one is suppressing the other. Our mind is our self. We cannot suppress it. We must treat it with respect, with gentleness, and absolutely without violence. Since we do not even know what our "self" is, how can we know if it is true or false, and whether or what to suppress? The only thing we can do is to let the sunlight of awareness shine on our "self" and enlighten it, so we can look at it directly.

Just as flowers and leaves are only part of a plant, and just as waves are only part of the ocean, perceptions, feelings, and thoughts are only part of the self. Blossoms and leaves are a natural manifestation of plants, and waves are a natural expression of oceans. It is useless to try to repress or stifle them. It is impossible. We can only observe them. Because they exist, we can find their source, which is exactly the same as our own.

The sun of awareness originates in the heart of the self. It enables the self to illuminate the self. It lights not only all thoughts and feelings present. It lights itself as well.

Let us return to the apple juice, quietly "resting." The river of our perceptions continues to flow, but now, in the sunlight of awareness, it flows peacefully, and we are serene. The relation between the river of perceptions and the sun of awareness is not the same as that of an actual river and the actual sun. Whether it is midnight or noon, whether the sun is absent or its penetrating rays are beaming down, the waters of the Mississippi River continue to flow, more or less the same. But when the sun of awareness shines on the river of our perceptions, the mind is transformed. Both river and sun are of the same nature.

Let us consider the relationship between the color of leaves and sunlight, which also have the same nature. At midnight, the starlight and moonlight reveal only the form of the trees and leaves. But if the sun were suddenly to shine, the green color of the leaves would immediately appear. The tender green of the leaves in April exists because the sunlight exists. One day, while sitting in a forest, mimicking the Prajñaparamita Heart Sutra, I wrote:

> Sunshine is green leaves.
> Green leaves are sunshine.
> Sunshine is not different from green leaves.
> Green leaves are not different from sunshine.
> The same is true of all forms and colors.[2]

As soon as the sun of awareness shines, at that very moment a great change takes place. Meditation lets the sun of awareness rise easily, so we can see more clearly. When we meditate, we seem to have two selves. One is the flowing river of thoughts and feelings, and the other is the sun of awareness that shines on them. Which is our own self? Which is true? Which false? Which is good? Which bad? Please calm down, my friend. Lay down your sharp sword of conceptual thinking. Don't be in such a hurry to cut your "self" in two. Both are self. Neither is true. Neither is false. They are both true and both false.

We know that light and color are not separate phenomena. In the same way, the sun of self and the river of self are not different. Sit with me, let a smile form on your lips, let your sun shine; close your eyes, if need be, to see your self more clearly. Your sun of awareness is only part of your river of self, isn't it? It follows the same laws as all psychological phenomena: it arises and vanishes away. To examine something with a microscope, a scientist must shine light on the object being observed. To observe the self, you must shine light on it too, the light of awareness.

I just told you to put down your sword of conceptualization and not cut your self into sections. Actually, you couldn't, even if you wanted to. Do you think you can separate the sunshine from the green color of the leaves? You can no more separate the observing self from the self observed. When the sun of awareness shines, the nature of thoughts and feelings is transformed. It is one with the observing mind, but they remain different, like the green of leaves and the sunshine. Don't rush from the concept of "two" to the concept of "one." This ever-present sun of awareness is at the same time its own object. When a lamp is turned on, the lamp itself is also brought to light. "I know that I know." "I am conscious of being conscious." When you think, "The sun of awareness has gone out in me," at that moment it relights itself, faster than the speed of light.

Darkness Becomes Light

Observe the changes that take place in your mind under the light of awareness. Even your breathing has changed and become "not-two" (I don't want to say "one") with your observing self. This is also true of your thoughts and feelings, which, together with their effects, are suddenly transformed. When you do not try to judge or suppress them, they become intertwined with the observing mind.

From time to time you may become restless, and the restlessness will not go away. At such times, just sit quietly, follow your breathing, smile a half-smile, and shine your awareness on the restlessness. Don't judge it or try to destroy it, because this restlessness is you yourself. It is born, has some period of existence, and fades away, quite naturally. Don't be in too big a hurry to find its source. Don't try too hard to make it disappear. Just illuminate it. You will see that little by little it will change, merging, becoming connected with you, the observer. Any psychological state that you subject to this illumination will eventually soften and acquire the same nature as the observing mind.

Throughout your meditation, keep the sun of your awareness shining. Like the physical sun, which lights every leaf and every blade of grass, our awareness lights our every thought and feeling, allowing us to recognize them, be aware of their birth, duration, and dissolution, without judging or evaluating, welcoming or banishing them. It is important that you do not consider awareness to be your "ally," called on to suppress the "enemies" that are your unruly thoughts. Do not turn your mind into a battlefield. Do not have a war there; for *all* your feelings—joy, sorrow, anger, hatred—are part of yourself. Awareness is like an elder brother or sister, gentle and attentive, who is there to guide and enlighten. It is a tolerant and lucid presence, never violent or discriminating. It is there to recognize and identify thoughts and feelings, not to judge them as good or bad, or place them into opposing camps in order to fight with each other. Opposition between good and bad is often compared to light and dark, but if we look at it in a different way, we will see that when light shines, darkness does not disappear. It doesn't leave; it merges with the light. It becomes the light.

A while ago I invited my guest to smile. To meditate does not mean to fight with a problem. To meditate means to observe. Your smile proves it. It proves that you are being gentle with yourself, that the sun of awareness is shining in you, that you have control of your situation. You are yourself, and you have acquired some peace. It is this peace that makes a child love to be near you.

A Poem for Buttoning Your Jacket

We can be better than a glass of apple juice. Not only can we settle peacefully while sitting still, we can also do it while standing, lying down, walking, or even working. What prevents you from allowing the sun of awareness to shine while you take a walk, make a cup of tea or coffee, or wash your clothes? When I first became a student at the Tu Hieu Monastery, I learned to maintain awareness during all activities—weeding the garden, raking leaves around the pond, washing dishes in the kitchen. I practiced mindfulness in the way taught by Zen Master Doc The in his little manual, *Essentials of the Practice to Apply Each Day*. According to this small book, we must be fully aware of all our actions. While waking up we know that we are waking up; while buttoning our jacket, we know that we are buttoning our jacket; while washing our hands we know that we are washing our hands. Master Doc The composed short poems for us to recite while washing our hands or buttoning our jacket, to help us remain firmly rooted in awareness. Here is the poem he wrote for us to recite while buttoning our jacket:

> While buttoning my jacket
> I hope that all beings
> Will keep their hearts warm
> And not lose themselves.

With the aid of verses like this, it is easy for the sun of awareness to shine its light on our physical actions as well as our thoughts and feelings. When I was a child I often heard my mother tell my elder sister that a girl must pay attention to her every movement. I was glad I was a boy who didn't have to pay attention like that. It was only when I began to practice meditation that I realized that I had to pay a thousand times more attention to my movements than my sister had. And not only to my movements, but also to my thoughts and feelings! My mother, like all mothers, knew that a girl who pays attention to her movements becomes more beautiful. Her movements are not jerky, rushed, or clumsy; they become gentle, calm, and graceful. Without knowing it, my mother taught my sister meditation.

In the same way, someone who practices awareness becomes beautiful to see. A Zen master, observing a student ringing the bell, sweeping the yard, setting the table, can guess how ripe that student is, can measure the student's "level of meditation" in his or her manners and personality. This "level" is the fruit of the practice of awareness, and the master calls it "the flavor of Zen."

Three Hours for a Cup of Tea

The secret of meditation is to be conscious of each second of your existence and to keep the sun of awareness continually shining—in both the physical and psychological realms, in all circumstances, on each thing that arises. While drinking a cup of tea, our mind must be fully present in the act of drinking the tea. Drinking tea or coffee can be one of our daily pleasures if we partake of it fully. How much time do you set aside for one cup of tea? In coffee shops in New York or Tokyo, people come in, order their coffee, drink it quickly, pay, and rush out to do something else. This takes a few minutes at most. Often there is loud music playing, and your ears hear the music, your eyes watch others gulping down their coffee, and your mind is thinking of what to do next. You can't really call this drinking coffee.

Have you ever participated in a tea ceremony? It may take two or three hours just being together and drinking one or two cups of tea. The time is not spent talking—only being together and drinking tea. Perhaps you think this is irresponsible because the participants are not worrying about the world situation, but you must admit that people who spend their time this way know how to drink tea, know the pleasure of having tea with a friend.

Devoting two hours to a cup of tea is, I agree, a little extreme. There are many other things to do: gardening, laundry, washing dishes, binding books, writing. Perhaps these other tasks are less pleasant than drinking tea or walking in the hills, but if we do them in full awareness, we will find them quite agreeable. Even washing the dishes after a big meal can be a joy.

Bathing a Newborn Buddha

To my mind, the idea that doing dishes is unpleasant can occur only when you aren't doing them. Once you are standing in front of the sink with your sleeves rolled up and your hands in warm water, it really isn't so bad. I enjoy taking my time with each dish, being fully aware of the dish, the water, and each movement of my hands. I know that if I hurry in order to go and have a cup of tea, the time will be unpleasant, and not worth living. That would be a pity, for each minute, each second of life is a miracle. The dishes themselves and the fact that I am here washing them are miracles! Each bowl I wash, each poem I compose, each time I invite a bell to sound is a miracle, and each has exactly the same value. One day, while washing a bowl, I felt that my movements were as sacred and respectful as bathing a newborn Buddha. If he were to read this, that newborn Buddha would certainly be happy for me, and not at all insulted at being compared with a bowl.

Each thought, each action in the sunlight of awareness becomes sacred. In this light, no boundary exists between the sacred and the profane. I must confess it takes me a bit longer to do the dishes, but I live fully in every moment, and I am happy. Washing the dishes is at the same time a means and an end, that is, not only do we do the dishes in order to have clean dishes, we also do the dishes just to do the dishes, to live fully in each moment while washing them.

If I am incapable of washing dishes joyfully, if I want to finish them quickly so I can go and have a cup of tea, I will be equally incapable of drinking the tea joyfully. With the cup in my hands I will be thinking about what to do next, and the fragrance and the flavor of the tea, together with the pleasure of drinking it, will be lost. I will always be dragged into the future, never able to live in the present moment.

Nourishing Awareness While Working

Our work, which lets us "earn our daily bread," can be done in the same way as the dishes. In my community, I bind books. Using a toothbrush, a small wheel, and a very heavy fireproof brick (about four or five pounds), I can bind two hundred books in a day. Before binding, I gather all the pages and arrange them numerically around a long table. Then I walk around the table, and when I have walked all around it, I know that I have the correct number of pages for one signature. Walking around the table, I know that I am not going anywhere in particular, so I walk slowly, gathering each page, conscious of each movement, breathing softly, conscious of each breath. I am at peace while assembling the pages, gluing them, and putting the cover on the book. I know I cannot produce as many books in a day as a professional bookbinder or a machine, but I also know that I do not hate my job. If you want a lot of money to spend, you must work hard and quickly, but if you live simply, you can work gently and in full awareness. I know many young people who prefer to work less, perhaps four hours a day, earning a small livelihood, so they can live simply and happily. This may be a solution to our society's problems—reducing the production of useless goods, sharing work with those who have none, and living simply and happily. Some individuals and communities have already proved that it is possible. This is a promising sign for the future, isn't it?

You may ask how you can nourish awareness while washing dishes, binding books, or working in a factory or an office. I think you have to find your own answer. Do whatever you can to keep the light of awareness shining inside yourself. You will discover ways that suit you, or you can try some techniques that others have tried—like reciting the short poems of Zen Master Doc The or concentrating on your breathing. You can maintain awareness of each inhalation and exhalation, of each movement of your lungs. When a thought or feeling arises, allow it to flow naturally with your breath. It may help to breathe lightly and a little more slowly than usual as a reminder that you are following your breathing.

The Precious Smile

While following your breathing you have been able to stay fully conscious for some time. You have succeeded a bit, haven't you? So why not smile? A tiny bud of a smile, just to prove you have succeeded. Seeing you smile, I know immediately that you are dwelling in awareness. Keep this smile always blooming, the half-smile of a buddha.

This tiny budding smile, how many artists have labored to bring it to the lips of countless statues of the Buddha? Perhaps you have seen them on the faces at Angkor Wat in Kampuchea, or those from Gandhara in northwest India. I am sure the same smile must have been on the faces of the sculptors as they worked. Can you imagine an angry sculptor giving birth to such a smile? Surely not! I know the sculptor who created the Parinirvana statue on Tra Cu Mountain in Vietnam. During the six months it took him to create that statue, he remained vegetarian, practicing sitting meditation, and studying sutras. Mona Lisa's smile is light, just a hint of a smile. Yet even a smile like that is enough to relax all the muscles on your face, to banish all worries and fatigue. A tiny bud of a smile on your lips nourishes awareness and calms you miraculously. It returns you to the peace you had lost.

When you walk in the hills, or in a park, or along a riverbank, you can follow your breath, with a half-smile blooming on your lips. When you feel tired or irritated, you can lie down with your arms at your sides, allowing all your muscles to relax, maintaining awareness of just your breath and your smile. Relaxing in this way is wonderful, and quite refreshing. You will benefit a lot if you practice it several times a day. Your mindful breath and your smile will bring happiness to you and to those around you. Even if you spend a lot of money on gifts for everyone in your family, nothing you could buy them can give as much true happiness as your gift of awareness, breathing, and smiling, and these precious gifts cost nothing.

Breathing Rhythmically

When you are too restless or under too much strain to follow your breathing, you can count your breath instead. Count "one" during the first inhalation and exhalation. Do not lose the thought "one." During the next inhalation and exhalation, count "two," and do not lose it. Continue on this way until you reach "ten," and then start again with "one." If you lose the thread of concentration at any time, you can start again at "one." When you are calm and concentrated, you will be able to follow your breath without counting.

Have you ever cut grass with a scythe? Some years ago, I brought a scythe home and tried to cut the grass around my cottage with it. It took more than a week before I found the best way to use it. The way you stand, the way you hold the scythe, the angle of the blade on the grass are all important. I found that if I coordinated the movement of my arms with the rhythm of my breathing and worked unhurriedly while maintaining awareness of my activity, I was able to work for a longer period of time. When I didn't do this, I became tired in just ten minutes. One day a Frenchman of Italian descent was visiting my neighbor, and I asked him to show me how to use a scythe. He was much more adept than I, but for the most part he used the same position and movements. What surprised me was that he too coordinated his movements with his breathing. Since then, whenever I see a neighbor cutting his grass with a scythe, I know he is practicing awareness.

Even before having a scythe, I used other tools—picks, shovels, rakes—coordinating my breath and my movement. I have found that except for very heavy labor, such as moving boulders or pushing full wheelbarrows (which make full awareness difficult), most jobs—turning the soil, making furrows, sowing seeds, spreading manure, watering—can be done in a relaxed and mindful way. During the past few years, I have avoided tiring myself and losing my breath. I think it is better not to mistreat my body. I must take care of it, treat it with respect as a musician does his instrument. I apply "nonviolence" to my body, for it is not merely a means to practice the Way, it is itself the Way. It is not only the temple, it is also the sage. I like and respect my gardening and bookbinding tools very much. I use them while following my breathing, and I feel that these tools and I breathe together in rhythm.

A Poem and a Peppermint Plant

I don't know what job you do every day, but I do know that some tasks lend themselves to awareness more easily than others. Writing, for example, is difficult to do mindfully. I have now reached the point when I know that a sentence is finished. But while writing the sentence, even now, I sometimes forget. That is why I have been doing more manual work and less writing these past few years. Someone said to me, "Planting tomatoes and lettuce may be the gateway to everything, but not everyone can write books and stories and poems as well as you do. Please don't waste your time with manual work!" I have not wasted any of my time. Planting a seed, washing a dish, cutting the grass are as eternal, as beautiful, as writing a poem! I do not understand how a poem can be better than a peppermint plant. Planting seeds gives me as much pleasure as writing a poem. For me, a head of lettuce or a peppermint plant has as much everlasting effect in time and space as a poem.

When I helped found the University of Advanced Buddhist Studies in 1964, I made a grave error. The students, who included young monks and nuns, studied only books, scriptures, and ideas. At the end, they had gathered nothing more than a handful of knowledge and their diploma. In the past, when novices were accepted into a monastery, they would be taken immediately into the garden to learn weeding, watering, and planting in full awareness. The first book they read was the collection of *gatha*s, or practice poems, by Master Doc The, the book that included the poems for buttoning your jacket, washing your hands, crossing a stream, carrying water, finding your slippers in the morning, and other practical things so they could practice awareness all day long. Only later would they begin to study sutras and participate in group discussions and private interviews with the master, and even then the scholarly studies would always go hand in hand with the practical ones. If I were to help found another university, I would model it on the old monasteries. It would be a community where all the students would eat, sleep, work, and live everyday life in the sunlight of awareness, perhaps like the Ark Community (L'Arche) in France or the Shanti Niketan or Phuong Boi communities. I am sure that in all the world's religions, meditation and study centers resemble one another. These are good models for universities as well.

Establishing a Spiritual Homeland

Each of us needs to "belong" to a place, such as a retreat center or a monastery, where each feature of the landscape, the sound of the bell, and even the buildings are designed to remind us to return to awareness. It is helpful to go there from time to time for several days or several weeks to renew ourselves. Even when we cannot actually go there, we only need to think of it, and we can feel ourselves smile and become peaceful and happy.

The people who live there should emanate peace and freshness, the fruits of living in awareness. They must always be there to care for us, console and support us, help us heal our wounds. Each of us must find a spiritual homeland where we can retreat from time to time, much as we ran to our mothers for refuge when we were young.

In the late 1950s, several of us built the Fragrant Palm Hermitage (Phuong Boi) in the Dalat Forest in central Vietnam. It was our spiritual homeland. Later, when some of us left to form La Boi Press, the School of Youth for Social Service, Van Hanh University, and Thuong Chieu Monastery, we were able to recall Phuong Boi and make each of these new institutions in its own way a spiritual homeland. Many of you are involved in working for social change and have a great need for such a healing place. When we were prevented by the war from returning to Phuong Boi, we went to Thuong Chieu Monastery, and when Thuong Chieu became inaccessible, we prepared for the birth of Plum Village in France.

Singing, Really Singing

We lead extremely busy lives. Even though we do not have to do as much manual labor as people in former times, we never seem to have enough time for ourselves. I know people who say they do not even have enough time to eat or breathe, and it appears to me to be true! What can we do about this? Can we take hold of time with both hands and slow it down?

First, let us light the torch of our awareness and learn again how to drink tea, eat, wash dishes, walk, sit, drive, and work in awareness. We do not have to be swept along by circumstances. We are not just a leaf or a log in a rushing river. With awareness, each of our daily acts takes on a new meaning, and we discover that we are more than machines, that our activities are not just mindless repetitions. We find that life is a miracle, the universe is a miracle, and we too are a miracle.

When we are invaded by confusion and dispersion, we can ask ourselves, "What exactly am I doing right now? Am I wasting my life?" These questions immediately relight our awareness and return our attention to our breathing. A small smile naturally appears on our lips, and each second of our work becomes alive. If you want to sing, please sing! Really sing!

From Sleep to Awakening

A political science professor asked me what I think about when I meditate. I told him, "I don't think about anything." I said that I am only attentive to what is there, what is going on. He appeared skeptical, but it is the truth. While sitting, I make almost no use of my intellect. I don't try to analyze things or solve complex problems, like math problems or riddles. Even if I am examining a *kung-an* (Japanese: *koan*), I just allow it to be there and I contemplate it, without seeking to explain or interpret it, because I know that a kung-an is not a puzzle to solve. Examination, in the sense of awareness, does not mean analysis. It only means continuous recognition. Thinking requires strenuous mental work, and makes us tired. This is not the case while resting in awareness or "recognizing." We have a tendency to think that meditation demands a great mobilization of "gray matter," but that is really not the case. A meditator is not a thinker; a meditator does not do mental labor. On the contrary, meditation rests the mind.

Since our conversation began with the apple juice, I haven't once asked my friend to use his "gray matter." I have only invited him to "see," to "recognize" things with me. To do that, we must concentrate, but not analyze. We must be attentive, without speculation or interpretation. Being attentive means giving only bare attention. It is a vehicle that can take you from sleep to awakening. If you do not *know* you are angry, feeling, thinking, sitting, and so forth, you are asleep. In his novel *The Stranger*, Albert Camus describes his anti-hero as a man who "lives as though dead." This is like living in a dark room with no light of awareness. When you light the lamp of awareness, you pass from sleep to awakening. The verb *budh* in Sanskrit means "to wake up," and one who wakes up is called a buddha. A buddha is a person who is always awake. From time to time we have this awareness, so we are "from-time-to-time" buddhas.

Awareness, Concentration, Understanding

"Awareness" (*sati* in Pali, *smrti* in Sanskrit) simply means being conscious of, remembering, or becoming acquainted with. But we must use it in the sense of being in the process of being conscious of, or being in the process of remembering. We have learned the word "awareness" in the sense of recognition, or bare attention, but the meaning doesn't stop there. In awareness, there are also the elements concentration (*samadhi*) and understanding (*prajña*). Concentration and understanding together are both the intensity of awareness and the fruit of awareness. Every time the lamp of awareness is lit, concentration (one-pointedness) and understanding (clear-seeing) are naturally present. The words "concentration" and "understanding" are often used as terms of consequence or effect. In terms of antecedent or cause, we may use the words "stopping" and "looking." If we can stop and look attentively, we succeed in seeing clearly. But what has to stop? Forgetfulness, dispersion, and confusion—the state of lost awareness, the absence of consciousness must stop. Stopping does not mean suppression. There is only the transformation of forgetfulness into remembrance, the absence of awareness into the presence of awareness.[3]

Cooking a Pot of Corn

The practice of meditation is not an exercise in analysis or reasoning. The sword of logic has no place in the practices of awareness, concentration, and understanding, or those of stopping and looking. In Vietnam, when we cook a pot of dried corn, we concentrate the fire under the pot and several hours later the kernels come loose and split open. When the sun's rays beat down on the snow, the snow slowly melts. When a hen sits on her eggs, the chicks inside gradually take form until they are ready to peck their way out. These are images that illustrate the effect of practicing meditation.

The aim of this practice is to see the true face of reality, which is mind and mind-object. When we speak of mind and of the outside world, we immediately are caught in a dualistic conception of the universe. If we use the words "mind" and "mind-object," we can avoid the damage done by the sword of conceptualized discrimination. The effect of meditation is like the fire under the pot, the sun's rays on the snow, and the hen's warmth on her eggs. In these three cases, there is no attempt at reasoning or analysis, just patient and continuous concentration. We can allow the truth to appear, but we cannot describe it using math, geometry, philosophy, or any other image of our intellect.

Examining a Kung-an

"Truth cannot be captured by concepts." I wonder who said this first. We too have this perception when we concentrate ourselves in order to observe. The sword of conceptual thinking only cuts truth into small, lifeless pieces all seemingly independent of each other. Many scientists acknowledge that great discoveries are often realized through intuition. For them, reason is not an agent of discovery but a tool to explain and support it afterward. These discoveries often occur at the most unexpected times, times when the scientist is not actively engaged in thinking, analyzing, or reasoning. An illuminating perception comes about because the scientist has been paying continual silent attention to the problem—while eating, walking, talking, even sleeping, every moment of the day. People working with kung-ans do so in exactly the same way. We speak of "meditating on" a kung-an, but a more precise description would be "examining" or "looking at" it. All the problems of life, all feelings such as passion, hatred, sadness, and suffering, as well as thoughts such as birth, death, form, emptiness, existence, and nonexistence can be used equally well as "objects of examination."

Awareness Is Both Cause and Effect

Awareness is at the same time cause and effect, concentration and understanding, stopping and looking. As soon as the light of awareness is lit, we concentrate, we are peaceful, we see ourselves more clearly. When a generator is running, the current flows and the bulb lights. When it keeps running while charging a battery, energy accumulates and charges the battery. In the same way, when awareness is maintained continuously, concentration and understanding accumulate. This is what we call "working intensively." Even in sleep, awareness does not cease and the kung-an continues to be examined, even without the knowledge of the sleeper. Sometimes we even continue in awareness while dreaming. When I practice intensively, I can see even in my dreams that I maintain awareness.

Conceiving the Inconceivable

The scientific method involves limiting as much as possible the field of observation in order to see clearly. The smaller the field, the greater the attention. However, at the level of subatomic particles, scientists have discovered that each particle is affected by all other particles, and even by the mind of the observing scientist. A school of theoretical physicists has developed the "bootstrap" concept, which suggests that every thing and every being in the universe depends on every other thing and every other being for its existence. We are used to believing that particles form "things," but in fact all particles are dependent upon all other particles and none has a separate individuality—"every particle is made up of all the others." This concept is quite similar to that expressed in the Avatamsaka Sutra, "All is one."[4]

If reality is an interaction, an "interbeing," how can we penetrate its essence? The *Tsao-tung* (Japanese: *Soto*) Zen sect teaches its practitioners just to observe, without judgment, without speculation. They say, "How can one conceive the inconceivable? Not thinking, that is the essence of Zen."[5] I like the Vietnamese words *quan chieu* because they include the idea of shining light on something in order to look at it—a looking free of all speculation, reasoning, interpretation, or evaluation. When the sun shines continuously on a lotus flower, it opens widely, revealing its seed-heart. In the same way, through the activity of looking, reality gently reveals itself. In meditation, the subject and object of pure observation are inseparable.

A Grain of Salt Enters the Sea

In science before the twentieth century, a line was always drawn between the researcher and the object of his or her study. Even today, except in the atomic realm, this is often true. A virologist and the virus under the microscope are regarded as two separate and independent entities.[6]

The attitude of meditation is exactly the opposite. Remember the relationship between the sunshine and the green leaf. When we illuminate something with our awareness, it changes, it blends and merges with the awareness. For example, when you are aware that you are happy, you may say, "I am aware that I am happy." If you go a step further, you may say, "I am aware of being aware that I am happy." There are three levels: The happiness, the awareness of happiness, and the awareness of being aware. I am offering this sword of conceptual thinking in order to demonstrate a point; but in truth, in you these three levels are one.

The Satipatthana Sutta, a Buddhist scripture that teaches awareness, uses expressions such as "observing the body in the body," "observing the feelings in the feelings," "observing the mind in the mind," "observing the objects of mind in the objects of mind."[7] Why are the words "body," "feelings," "mind," and "objects of mind" repeated? Some masters of the Abhidhamma say that the purpose of this repetition is to underline the importance of these words. I see it otherwise. I think that these words are repeated in order to remind us not to separate the meditator and the object of meditation. We must live with the object, identify with it, merge with it, like a grain of salt entering the sea in order to measure the saltiness of the sea.

It is the same with a kung-an. A kung-an is not a problem to be solved with the intellect. A kung-an is not a kung-an if it is someone else's. A kung-an is only a kung-an when it is our own. It must be our own question of life and death—it cannot be apart from our daily life. It must be planted in our flesh and bones; we must be the soil that nourishes it. Only then will its fruit and flowers be our own fruit and flowers.

The word "comprehend" is formed by combining two Latin roots: *com* (together) and *prehendere* (take, or grasp). To understand means *to take* something and *join together* with it. If we only analyze someone from the outside, without becoming one with them, without entering their shoes, their skin, we will never really understand them. The theologian Martin Buber has said that the relation between a person and God is not one of subject and object, because God cannot be the object of our knowledge. Twentieth-century physicists have come to realize that "no totally objective phenomenon can exist, that is to say, independent of the observer's mind. And correlatively, all subjective phenomena present an objective fact."[8]

The Dance of the Bees

Don't Leave Your Fate in the Hands of Others

ONE EVENING I RETURNED to my hermitage from a walk in the hills, and I found that all the doors and windows of the hermitage had been blown open. When I left the house, I hadn't secured them, and a cold wind blew through the house, opened the windows, and scattered the papers from my desk all over the room. Immediately I closed the doors and windows, lit a lamp, picked up the papers, and arranged them neatly on my desk. Then I started a fire in the fireplace, and soon the crackling logs brought warmth back to the room.

Sometimes in a crowd we feel tired, cold, and lonely. We may wish to withdraw to be by ourselves and become warm again, as I did at the hermitage, sitting by the fire, protected from the cold, damp wind. Our senses are our windows to the outside world, and sometimes the wind blows and disturbs everything within us. Many of us leave our windows open all the time, allowing the sights and sounds of the world to invade us, penetrate us, and expose our sad, troubled selves. We feel so cold and lonely and afraid. Do you ever find yourself watching an awful TV program, unable to turn it off? The raucous noises, explosions of gunfire, are upsetting. Yet you don't get up and turn it off. Why do you torture yourself in this way? Don't you want to close your windows? Are you afraid of solitude—the emptiness and the loneliness you may find when you face yourself alone?

We are what we feel and perceive. If we are angry, we are the anger. If we are in love, we are the love. If we look at a snowy mountain peak, we are the mountain. Watching a bad TV program, we are the TV program. While dreaming, we are the dream. We can be anything we want, even without a magic wand. So why do we open our windows to bad movies and TV programs, movies made by sensationalist producers in search of easy money, movies which make our hearts pound, our fists tighten, and send us back into the streets exhausted? Who allows such movies and TV programs to be made? Especially for the very young? We do! We are too undemanding, too ready to watch whatever is on the screen, too lonely, lazy, or bored to create our own lives. We turn on the TV and leave it on, allowing someone else to guide us, shape us, and destroy us. Losing ourselves in this way is leaving our fate in the hands of others who may not be acting responsibly. We must be aware of what kinds of programs do harm to our nervous systems, our minds, and our hearts, and which programs and films benefit us.

I am not just talking about movies and TV programs. All around us, how many lures are set there by our fellows and ourselves? In a single day, how many times do we become lost and scattered because of them? We must be very careful to protect our fate and our peace. That does not mean shutting all our windows, for there are many miracles in the world we call "outside." Open your windows to these miracles. Look at any one of them with the light of awareness. Even while sitting beside a clear, flowing stream, listening to beautiful music, or watching an excellent movie, do not entrust yourself entirely to the stream, the music, or the film. Continue to be aware of yourself and your breathing. With the sun of awareness shining in us, we can avoid most dangers—the stream will be purer, the music more harmonious, and the soul of the artist completely visible in the film.

A beginning meditator may want to leave the city and go off to the countryside to help close those windows that would trouble your spirit if left open. There you can become one with the quiet forest, and rediscover and restore yourself without being carried away by the chaos of "the outside world." The fresh and silent woods help you remain in awareness. When awareness is well rooted, when you can maintain it without faltering, then you may wish to return to the city and remain there, less troubled. But before you reach this point, you must be very careful, nourishing your awareness moment by moment, choosing the surroundings and sustenance that assist you the most.

Do Not Take a Cold Shower When You Have the Flu

If you are a professional critic, you read a book or watch a movie with an observing mind. While reading or watching you are aware of your responsibility as a critic and you do not become possessed by the book or film. You remain in control of yourself. When you live in awareness, you also remain in control of yourself. Though your windows are open on the world, you are not compelled by it. If we need to protect our senses, it is because we are not yet strong enough to fully encounter the world, just as someone with a cold or the flu may not be strong enough to take a cold shower.

I remember one day at La Boi Press, a small book publishing company several of us started in Vietnam, I was invited to say something about arts and letters. I said that they must both reveal and heal. To reveal means to show the true situation of people and society. To heal means to show ways to cure them. The Buddha is often called the Medicine King because his teaching is adapted to each particular being and situation. Prince Siddhartha retired to the forest to sit beside a stream for many years before returning to the world of people. Today we live in noisy and polluted societies, filled with injustice, but we can take refuge in a public park or along a riverbank for a moment. Contemporary music, literature, and entertainment do little to help with healing; to the contrary, much of it compounds the bitterness, desperation, and weariness we all feel. We need to find ways to protect ourselves, to learn when to open and when to close our sense-windows. This is the first step for a beginning meditator.

I find that I need surroundings and objects that fit me, that contribute to my happiness, peace, and health. Where are they? They are right there in the "outside world." A stream in a forest, the eyes of a child, a dear friend, an excellent book, a concert, a delicious, healthy meal, I know these things are available. But without awareness, I am not fully able to enjoy and appreciate them.

Taking Care of the Apple Tree in Your Yard

As we sit down next to a stream, we can listen to its laughter and watch its sparkling waters, noticing the pebbles glistening and the fresh green plants nearby, and we may be overcome with happiness. We are one with the stream's freshness, purity, and clarity. But in just an instant we may find we've had enough. Our heart is troubled, and we think of other things. We are no longer at one with the stream. It is of no use to sit in a peaceful forest if our mind is lost in the city. When we live with a child or a friend, their freshness and warmth can relax us. But if our heart is not with them, their precious presence is neglected, and they no longer exist. We must be aware of them to appreciate their value, to allow them to be our happiness. If through carelessness and forgetfulness we become dissatisfied with them, and begin asking too much of them or reprimanding them, we will lose them. Only after they are gone will we realize their preciousness and feel regret. But once they are gone, all our regrets are in vain.

Around us, life bursts forth with miracles—a glass of water, a ray of sunshine, a leaf, a caterpillar, a flower, laughter, raindrops. If you live in awareness, it is easy to

see miracles everywhere. Each human being is a multiplicity of miracles. Eyes that see thousands of colors, shapes,
and forms; ears that hear a bee flying or a thunderclap; a
brain that ponders a speck of dust as easily as the entire
cosmos; a heart that beats in rhythm with the heartbeat
of all beings. When we are tired and feel discouraged by
life's daily struggles, we may not notice these miracles,
but they are always there.

Have a look at the apple tree in your yard. Look at it
with complete attention. It is truly a miracle. If you notice
it, you will take good care of it, and you too are part of its
miraculousness. Even after caring for it for only a week,
its leaves are already greener and shinier. It is exactly
the same with the people who are around you. Under
the influence of awareness, you become more attentive,
understanding, and loving, and your presence not only
nourishes you and makes you lovelier, it enhances them
as well. Our entire society can be changed by one person's
peaceful presence.

Our minds create everything. The majestic mountaintop, brilliant with snow, is you yourself when you contemplate it. Its existence depends on your awareness. When
you close your eyes, as long as your mind is present, the
mountain is there. Sitting in meditation, with several
sense-windows closed, you feel the presence of the whole
universe. Why? Because the mind is there. If your eyes
are closed, it is so that you can see better. The sights and
sounds of the world are not your enemies. Your enemy is
forgetfulness, the absence of mindfulness.

Don't Become a Colony

As I write, French workers are struggling to reduce their workweek from forty hours to thirty-five. They are working hard to accomplish this, but these five hours, how will they use them? If they use them the way they spend their Saturday nights, sitting at a bar or in front of a TV, it will be a terrible waste. We all need time to relax and to live, but how? Usually when we have some free time, we watch whatever is on TV in order to avoid "having nothing to do," which means staying home alone with ourselves. Watching TV may make us more tired, more nervous, more unbalanced, but we rarely notice these results. The free time we struggle so hard for is seized by TV broadcasting companies and the prod ucts of their advertisers. We end up being their colony. We have to find ways to use our precious time to rest and be happy.

We can choose good TV shows to watch, beautiful places to go, meetings with dear friends, books and records that suit us well. And we can live in a relaxed, contented way with what we have chosen. Remember, we are whatever we choose. Have you ever been on a beach when the sun rises, or on a mountaintop at noon? Did you stretch your arms wide and breathe deeply, filling your lungs with pure, clean air, with unbounded immensity? Did you feel as if you were just the sky, the sea, the mountain? If you are too far away from the sea or a mountain, you can sit cross-legged and breathe gently and deeply, and the sea, the mountain, the entire universe will enter you.

The Known Is Not Separate from the Knower

To be aware is to be aware of something. When the mind settles on the mountain, it becomes the mountain. When it settles on the sea, it becomes the sea. When we say "know," both the known and the knower are included. When we meditate on our body, we are our body; we limit our observations to our body, even though we realize that our body is not separate from the rest of the universe. If we meditate on limitless space, we become limitless space (*akasanantyayatana*). If we meditate on the consciousness that includes both space and time, we reach the state of limitless consciousness (*vijñananantyayatana*). If we meditate on the absence of identity of all things, we enter the state of nothingness (*akiñcanyayatana*). If we meditate on the non-distinction between knower and known, we come to the state of "neither perception nor non-perception" (*naivasañjñanasañjñayatana*). The Four Formless States of Consciousness are not as difficult to reach as you might think, provided awareness is there to shine on every movement of the mind.

You may try to experience one of these—which one is not important. The key point is to never let your awareness stand apart from whatever you regard as the object of awareness. Once you are aware, body, mountaintop, or flowing river all become your mind.

Letting Go of "In" and "Out"

You may have noticed that each time I use the expression "outside world," I put it in quotes. This is because to me it is not really "outside." Look deeply at this: Is the world outside your body? Is it outside your mind? Our body—blood, flesh, bones—belongs to this "outside world." In fact, our brain and nervous system do not escape it either. Perhaps the several hundred square centimeters that comprise our brain can be considered "inside." But no, the brain occupies space, and space is part of the "outside world," isn't it?

Is our mind in the "inner" world? Where is mind to be found? Can you identify it in space? No, all you can do is observe it, observe it observing itself. Please try looking at your mind as though it were something physical. We know that the mind is related to the brain and to the nervous system. It is memory, feeling, thought, perception, knowledge. These mental phenomena have physiological roots; they are born and they die; they have intensity. Can we locate them in space and time? In space, the nervous system serves as their base. In time, they may appear yesterday or today or tomorrow. So mind itself may be regarded as part of the so-called "outer" world. Continue to examine and you will find that everything seems to belong to the "outside world." But outside of what? How can there be an "outer" without an "inner"?

Do not jump to the conclusion that the "outer" world is located in the mind and that the mind encloses the entire universe. That conclusion continues to accept the distinction between "inside" and "outside." To say, "Everything is found inside the mind; there is nothing outside the mind," is as absurd as saying, "It is mind that realizes the outer world."

Our confusion stems from the habit of distinguishing "in" and "out." In normal daily life, this distinction is necessary. If we stay indoors, we may be comfortable dressing lightly, even on a cold winter day. But if we go outside without dressing more warmly, we may catch a cold. Concepts such as high and low, one and many, coming and going, birth and death, are all important in everyday life. But when we leave the realm of the practical to meditate on the true nature of the universe, we must also leave behind these concepts. For example, when you raise your eyes to look up at the stars and the moon, you say that they are "above." But at the very same moment, for someone standing on the opposite side of the planet, the direction you are looking is "below" for them. When looking at the entire universe, we have to abandon all these concepts of high and low, and so forth.

Reality Cannot Be Contained

Abandoning concepts is of prime importance for a meditator. When we observe our body, our feelings, our thoughts, our perceptions, we situate them in space and time just as when we observe physical phenomena. We see psychological phenomena and physical, physiological phenomena.

You may ask, "When mind becomes the object of its own observation, is that which is grasped mind itself or only a projection or reflection of mind?" This is a good question. You may also want to ask, "When physiological and physical phenomena are observed as objects, do they keep their true nature or do they become just a projection or reflection of reality, transformed by becoming objects of observation?" Our mind creates categories—space and time, above and below, inside and outside, myself and others, cause and effect, birth and death, one and many—and puts all physical and psychological phenomena into categories like these before examining them and trying to find their true nature. It is like filling many different shapes and sizes of bottles with water in order to find out the shape and size of water. Truth itself transcends these concepts, so if you want to penetrate it you must break all the conceptual categories you use in normal daily life. The Theory of Relativity recognizes that if you do not abandon the idea that space and time are absolute and independent of one another, you cannot make progress in understanding the universe. Quantum theory says that if you want to understand the world of subatomic particles, you must leave behind matter and empty space, cause and effect, front and back, concepts so useful in daily life.

Understanding Is the Fruit of Meditation, Not of Thought

Quantum theorists today know that the consciousness of the observer is in a very close relationship with the object observed, and they are directing more and more of their attention to that consciousness. In 1979, France-Culture organized a one-week meeting in Córdoba, Spain, on "Mind and Science." Many renowned scholars were present, and a number of them affirmed their conviction that the world and mind have the same nature.

Although some scientists have seen the fundamental characteristic of mind, I am afraid that most still want to study it like any other object in their laboratories. Then it is no longer mind, but the projection or reflection of it, framed by conceptions. Remember the phrase from the Satipatthana Sutta: "Observe the body in the body, observe the feelings in the feelings, observe the mind in the mind, observe the objects of mind in the objects of mind." This means that you must live in the body in full awareness of it, and not just study it like a separate object. Live in awareness with feelings, mind, and objects of mind. Do not just study them. When we meditate on our body, we live with it as truth and give it our most lucid attention; we become one with it. The flower blossoms because sunlight touches and warms its bud, becoming one with it. Meditation reveals not a concept of truth, but a direct view of truth itself. This we call Insight, the kind of understanding based on attention and concentration.

Thinking is to take cinder blocks of concepts from the memory warehouse and build monuments. We call these hovels and palaces "thoughts." But such thinking, by itself, has no creative value. It is only when lit by understanding that thinking takes on real substance. Understanding does not arise as a result of thinking. It is a result of the long process of conscious awareness. Sometimes understanding can be translated into thoughts, but often thoughts are too rigid and limited to carry much understanding. Sometimes a look or a laugh expresses understanding much better than words or thoughts.

The Dance of the Bees

Have you ever read a book or seen a film about bees? When a worker bee finds a hillside covered with flowers, she flies back to the hive to tell her mates exactly where the flowers are, and she does it with a dance. She can even tell them of places quite far away. Karl von Frisch revealed this to us after studying the language of the dance of the bees.[1]

We humans also know how to dance. Some of us dance with our bodies, others with painting or music. Even our spoken and written words are no more than the steps of a dance, the notes of a song, the strokes of a painting. They may be more or less skillful. They may translate our vision poorly or well. The skill is not only in the hands of the artist or the words of the speaker; the listener too must be skillful and perceptive. With words it is especially difficult to escape from conceptual categorizations; and even if the speaker skillfully avoids them, the listener can still fall into their traps. Remember the empty bottles? They had definite shapes and sizes even before being filled. People who practice Zen often advise not using words. This is not to discredit words, but to avoid the danger of becoming stuck in them. It is to encourage us to use words as skillfully as possible for the sake of those who hear them.

In the second century, Nagarjuna wrote the Madhyamaka Sastra, in which he used concepts to destroy concepts. He was not trying to create a new doctrine, but to break *all* the bottles, *all* the flasks, *all* the vases, *all* the containers, to prove that water needs no form to exist. He outlined a dance for us, a dance for us to drop our categories and barriers so that we can directly encounter reality and not content ourselves with its mere reflection.

Knowledge Is a Barrier to Understanding

The great discoveries of science are the result of understanding rather than thought. Scientists' tools are not just their intellect and laboratory; their whole being down to its depths is hard at work. Intellect prepares the soil of the mind and sows the seeds there. Until the seeds sprout, intellect can do no more. To try would only be floundering in a void. Then, at unexpected moments, the seeds send shoots up into the intelligence. These moments usually come because the scientist has "hatched" them. He or she has "sat" on the problem while awake, asleep, eating, walking, until *suddenly a solution!* The new discovery breaks the old knowledge, and the intellect is forced to destroy today's structures to build tomorrow's. Old knowledge is the obstacle to new understanding; Buddhism calls it "the barrier built of knowledge." Like those who are awakened, great scientists have undergone great internal changes. If they are able to achieve profound realizations, it is because their powers of observation, concentration, and awareness are deeply developed.

Understanding is not an accumulation of knowledge. To the contrary, it is the result of the struggle to become free of knowledge. Understanding shatters old knowledge to make room for the new that accords better with reality. When Copernicus discovered that the earth goes around the sun, most of the astronomical knowledge of the time had to be discarded, including the ideas of above and below. Today, physics is struggling valiantly to free itself from the ideas of identity and cause/effect that underlie classical science. Science, like the Tao (Way), urges us to get rid of all preconceived notions.

When Shakyamuni Buddha put forth the notion of "not self," he upset many concepts about life and the universe. He blasted our most firm and widespread conviction—that of a permanent self. Those who understand "not self" know that its function is to overthrow "self," not to replace it with a new concept of reality. The notion of "not self" is a method, not a goal. If it becomes a concept, it must be destroyed along with all other concepts.

Unable to Describe It

Understanding, in humans, is translated into concepts, thoughts, and words. Understanding is not an aggregate of bits of knowledge. It is a direct and immediate penetration.

In the realm of sentiment, it is feeling. In the realm of intellect, it is perception. It is an intuition rather than the culmination of reasoning. Every now and again it is fully present in us, and we find we cannot express it in words, thoughts, or concepts. "Unable to describe it," that is our situation at such moments. Insights like this are spoken of in Buddhism as "impossible to reason about, to discuss, or to incorporate into doctrines or systems of thought."

Who Knows?

We boast of the knowledge that we, as humans, have achieved. These are the treasures of our species, transmitted since the beginning of time when we were "inorganic," on the edge of becoming "organic." When we discuss "knowing," we immediately think of humans with our large brains, forgetting that knowing is present in all species, even those we consider inanimate. Certainly, bees, spiders, and wasps, are highly skilled—they build beautiful structures. Looking at a beehive, a wasp's nest, or a spider's web, we admit their know-how, but we say, "These species do not know how to think. They cannot do mathematics. They cannot plan and design projects. They don't have intelligence. All they have is instinct." Still, it was not we humans who gave them nests and webs, it was the little "brainless" creatures themselves who designed and built those marvelous architectures that we so admire. If they do not *know*, who does? They know. Their species in its evolution has acquired this knowledge.

When we look at plants, we also see miracles of knowing. The apple tree *knows* how to make roots, branches, leaves, flowers, and fruit. You say that the apple tree, having no intelligence, has no other choice. But your ribs, your glands, your backbone, have you created them with your intelligence? It is the work of "knowing," which embraces all, including our ability to think.

Knowing in the Blue Sky

Let us try to move away from our notions of self and use a kind of language in which the subject is absent. For example, we say, "It is raining." "It" is the subject, but that really does not tell us anything. We may say, "The rain is falling." "Rain" is the subject and "is falling" the verb. But this sentence does not make much sense either, because when it is raining there must be water falling or it is not rain. So we can say, "Raining in London," or "Raining in Chicago," without using a subject, and the reality is clearly expressed.

Let us use the word "know" in this way. "Knowing in the person." "Knowing in the bee." "Knowing in the apple tree." It sounds strange because we are used to using a subject when we speak. The word "knowing" here can be either a subject or a verb, as in "raining in London" or "raining in Chicago." If "raining in London" means there is rain in London, then "knowing in the person" means there is knowledge in the person, nothing is obscured! To my mind, understanding is present everywhere, always unfolding. Knowing in Fred, knowing in Rachel, knowing in a bee, knowing in an apple tree, knowing in nothingness, knowing in the Milky Way. If we can say, "Raining in Chicago," there is no reason we cannot say, "Knowing in the blue sky."[2] While conducting a week-long retreat on the practice of not-self, a Zen master might propose to the retreatants that they use only this language, without subjects. I am sure this method would bear excellent results.

There Is Knowing in the Wind

Let us amuse ourselves for a moment with a dance, so that we can better understand "knowing." Suppose I say, "I know that it's windy." "I" refers more to my mind than my body, so this sentence really means, "My mind knows that it is windy." Mind is the knower, so really we are saying, "The knower knows that it is windy." "The knower" is the subject, "knows" is the verb, and "it is windy" is the object. But it is funny to say, "The knower knows," isn't it? We imagine that the knower is an entity which exists independently of its object and which resides in our brain making brief excursions into the "outside world" to see what is happening out there. Just as we use a ruler to measure something, we fit our mind to a preconceived model, one that was created by our mind itself. Therefore, what we call "mind" is not pure and true mind. It is enmeshed in concepts.

When we say, "I know the wind is blowing," we don't think that there is something blowing something else. "Wind" goes with "blowing." If there is no blowing, there is no wind. It is the same with knowing. Mind is the knower; the knower is mind. We are talking about knowing in relation to the wind. "To know" is to know something. Knowing is inseparable from the wind. Wind and knowing are one. We can say, "Wind," and that is enough. The presence of wind indicates the presence of knowing, and the presence of the action of blowing. If we reduce the sentence "I know the wind is blowing" to simply "Wind," we can avoid grammatical mistakes and approach reality. In daily life, we have grown used to a way of thinking and expressing ourselves that is based on the idea that everything is independent of everything else. This way of thinking and speaking makes it difficult to penetrate nondualistic, nondiscriminatory reality, a reality which cannot be contained in concepts.

Each Action Its Own Subject

The wind blows. The rain falls. The river flows. In sentences like these we can see clearly that the subject and the verb are one and the same. There is no wind without "blowing," no rain without "falling," no river without "flowing." If we look closely, we can see that the subject of the act is in the action, that the act itself is exactly its own subject.

The most universal verb is the verb *to be*: I am, you are, the mountain is, a river is. The verb "to be" does not express the dynamic living state of the universe. To express that we must say "become." These two verbs can also be used as nouns: "being," "becoming." But being what? Becoming what? "Becoming" means "evolving ceaselessly" and is as universal as the verb "to be." It is not possible to express the "being" of a phenomenon and its "becoming" as if the two were independent. In the case of wind, "blowing" is the being *and* the becoming. For rain, its being *and* becoming are "falling." For the river, its being *and* becoming are "flowing."

We say that "rain falls," but "fall" is not the most precise term. Snow, leaves, and even radiation also fall. If we say "to rain," that would be a more precise description for the activity of the subject "rain." We can say, "The rain rains," to describe this activity, using "rain" as both subject and verb. Or we can just say, "Raining," or even, "Rain." In the same way we can say, "The painter paints," "The reader reads," "The meditator meditates." Following this pattern of usage we can also say, "The king kings," "The mountain mountains," "The cloud clouds." The reason for the existence of the king is to be king, to act king. The reason for the existence of the mountain is to be, to act, to do mountain. "Acting-being" king means doing what a king does—reigning over the people, giving royal audiences, and a thousand other things. So, as in the case of "rain rains," we can simply say, "The king kings." Then the first word is the subject and the second the verb, a verb which is not universal, a verb which is used just for kings. Thus each subject becomes a verb, and the verb is the being of the subject. To our ears, "The painter paints," sounds

better than "The king kings"; but in fact there is no dif-
ference between them. Many, many years ago, Confucius
used this kind of language. He said, "King kings, subject
subjects, parent parents, child childs." That is, "The king
is-does king," "The subject is-does subject," and so on. We
can add further explanations, such as, "The king must do
his duty as a king," or "A king must serve sincerely as
king," but in the end these additions and embellishments
add nothing. When we have seen that each action is its
own subject, we can begin to comprehend the immense
application of the word "knowing."

Inanimate Objects, Do You Have a Soul?

We are so used to thinking of "knowing" in terms of
feelings and perceptions that we label inorganic objects
as "inanimate, insensitive, devoid of intelligence." But
these things are only inanimate from our point of view.
A rock is composed of countless molecules, which are in
turn composed of countless atomic and subatomic particles, which are all held together by electromagnetic and
nuclear forces. Atoms are not lifeless bits of solid, inert
matter. They are vast empty spaces in which infinitely
small particles (protons, electrons, neutrons, and so forth)
are in perpetual movement at enormous speeds. Why do
they act this way? Can we still say that a rock is "inert,
inanimate, insensitive"? The poet Lamartine once asked,
"Inanimate objects, do you have a soul?"[3] If we define soul
according to our ideas and beliefs, no doubt they haven't,

or at least, they do not manifest it. But in the sense of a dynamic, living reality, they surely do!

The Known Manifests Itself in Countless Ways

"Knowing" reveals itself in many ways. "Knowing" can be active whenever there is hearing, seeing, feeling, comparing, remembering, imagining, reflecting, worrying, hoping, and so forth. In the Vijñanavada school of Buddhism, which specialized in the study of "consciousnesses," many more fields of activity were attributed to knowing. For instance, in *alayavijñana*, or "store consciousness," the fields of activity of "knowing" are "maintaining, conserving, and manifesting." According to the Vijñanavadins, all sensation, perception, thought, and knowledge arise from this basic store consciousness. *Manyana* is one of the ways of knowing based on this consciousness, and its function is to grasp on to the object and take it as a "self." *Manovijñana* serves as the headquarters for all sensations, perceptions, and thoughts, and makes creation, imagination, as well as dissection of reality possible. *Amala* is the consciousness that shines like a pure white light on store consciousness.[4]

In any phenomenon, whether psychological, physiological, or physical, there is dynamic movement, life. We can say that this movement, this life, is the universal manifestation, the most commonly recognized action of knowing. We must not regard "knowing" as something from the outside which comes to breathe life into the universe. It is the life of the universe itself. The dance and the dancer are one.

Tasting Yourself at the Foot of an Apple Tree

You know, I haven't been saying all this just to provide amusement, juggling words and understanding for your entertainment. These are tools which we can use to shatter and demolish our habitual and troublesome ways of thinking, old habits forged by our everyday lives. These are chisels and crowbars and axes to dismantle our furniture or split trees into logs for the fire. To split a log, you must insert a wedge into a crack and hammer at it until the log gradually splits in two. In the same way, reading this may put a wedge in you, depending on your interest, and your meditation practice. If what I have been saying is not clear for you, it may be because you are not yet used to seeing in this upside-down way. It may be the first time you have been encouraged to examine reality with a nondiscriminatory spirit. Or it may be that my dancing is still too clumsy. It doesn't matter. We will try to find another way. If we cannot enter through one particular door, there are many others to try. In Buddhism it is said there are 84,000 doors to enter into the Dharma. I think we have to create even more. The point is to "see into" reality, not to understand what I am saying. My words can only be hints of an evocative dance, a pointing finger. You must see with your own eyes, eyes opened in full awareness.

I hope you are not going to transform my words into concepts, new concepts that can be stored inside you. I don't want to give you anything. I only want to dance for you, like the bee. If you see something, you must realize that you yourself have seen it. It is in you, not in my dance. Please go and sit next to a sleeping child. Look at the child. Or go into your yard and sit at the foot of an apple tree. Or go into the kitchen and make yourself a cup of tea. Whatever you do, do it in full attentiveness, in full awareness. Do not lose yourself in forgetfulness. Please don't think at all about becoming one with the child, the tree, the tea. There is no need to think at all. Taste yourself with the child, taste yourself with the tree, taste yourself with the tea while a smile blossoms on your lips.

The Universe in a Speck of Dust

Mind and Object Are One

THE OTHER AFTERNOON, when I returned to my hermitage, I closed all the doors and windows because it was so windy. This morning, my window is open and I can see the cool, green forest. The sun is shining and a bird is singing beautifully. Little Thuy has already left for school. I must stop writing for a moment so I can look at the trees stretching across the hillside. I am aware of their presence and my own presence. It is not always necessary to close our sense-doors in order to be concentrated. Beginning meditators, to make concentrating on their breath or another object easier, may find it beneficial to close their sight and sound windows, but concentration is also possible with these windows open. Sense objects do not exist just outside the body. Even while we are not seeing, hearing, smelling, or tasting, we cannot ignore the feelings inside our bodies. When you have a toothache, or a cramp in your leg, you feel the pain. When all your organs are healthy, you feel a sense of well-being. Buddhism speaks of three kinds of feelings: pleasant, unpleasant, and neutral. But really, so-called neutral feelings can be quite pleasant, if we are aware.

The feelings inside the body are an uninterrupted stream, whether we are aware of them or not, so to "close all our sense-doors" is actually impossible. Even if we were somehow able to barricade them, the mind and consciousness would continue to work, and we would have images, concepts, and thoughts arising from memory. Some people think that to meditate is to separate ourselves from the world of thoughts and feelings and return to a kind of pure state where the mind contemplates itself and becomes "true mind."[1] It is a lovely idea, but it is basically misleading. Since mind is not separate from the world of thoughts and feelings, how can it leave and retire into itself? When I look at the trees in front of me, my mind does not go outside of me into the forest, nor does it open a door to let the trees in. My mind fixes on the trees, but they are not a distinct object. My mind and the trees are one. The trees are only one of the miraculous manifestations of the mind.

> Forest.
> Thousands of tree-bodies and mine.
> Leaves are waving,
> ears hear the stream's call,
> eyes see into the sky of mind,
> a half-smile unfolds on every leaf.
> There is a forest here
> because I am here.
> But mind has followed the forest
> and clothed itself in green.

The sage enters samadhi, and he or she does not know there is an "outside world" to keep out or an "inside world" to penetrate. The world reveals itself, even when the eyes are closed. The world is neither inner nor outer. It is vital and complete in any object of contemplation—the breath, the tip of the nose, a kung-an, or anything else, as tiny as a speck of dust or as huge as a mountain. Whatever the object, it is not fragmented from ultimate reality. In fact, it contains the vast totality of reality.

Small Is Not Inside, Big Is Not Outside

I invite you to meditate with me. Please sit in a position that you find relaxing, so that you are comfortable, and place your attention on your breathing, letting it become very gentle, very light. After a few moments, move your attention to the feelings in your body. If you feel any pain or discomfort, or if you feel anything pleasurable, bring your attention there and enjoy that feeling with all of your awakened consciousness. After a little while, notice the functioning of your different organs—your heart, lungs, liver, kidneys, digestive system, and so forth. Normally these organs function without difficulty and do not attract your attention unless they are in pain. Notice the blood flowing like a river through the countryside, nourishing the fields with fresh water.

You know that this river of blood nourishes all the cells of your body and that your organs, composed of cells, enrich (digestive system), purify (liver, lungs), and propel (heart) the blood. All the body's organs, including the nervous system and glands, rely on each other for existence. Lungs are necessary for blood, so lungs belong to blood. Blood is necessary to lungs, so blood belongs to lungs. In the same way we can say lungs belong to heart, liver belongs to lungs, and so forth, and we see that every organ in the body implies the existence of all the others. This is called "the interdependence of all things," or "interbeing" in the Avatamsaka Sutra. Cause and effect are no longer perceived as linear, but as a net, not a two-dimensional one, but a system of countless nets interwoven in all directions in multidimensional space. Not only does each organ contain in itself the existence of all the other organs, but each cell contains in itself all the other cells. One is present in all and all are present in each one. This is expressed clearly in the Avatamsaka Sutra as, "One is all, all is one."

When we fully grasp this, we are freed from the pitfall of thinking of "one" and "many," a habit that has held us trapped for so long. When I say, "One cell contains in itself all the other cells," do not misunderstand me and think that there is some way that one cell's capacity can be stretched to fit all the others inside of it. I mean that the presence of one cell implies the presence of all the others, since they cannot exist independently, separate from the others. A Vietnamese Zen master once said, "If this speck of dust did not exist, the entire universe could not exist."[2] Looking at a speck of dust, an awakened person sees the universe. Beginners in meditation, although they do not see this as clearly as an apple in their hand, are able to understand it with observation and reflection. The Avatamsaka Sutra contains phrases that can terrify and confuse readers who have not meditated on the principle of interdependence. "In every speck of dust I see innumerable Buddha worlds, in each of these worlds countless Buddhas shining, their precious auras shining." "Putting one world in all worlds, putting all worlds in one world." "Innumerable Sumeru Mountains can be hung on the end of a hair." In the phenomenal world, things seem to exist as separate entities which have a specific place: "This" is on the outside of "that." When we deeply penetrate the principle of interdependence, we see that this sense of separateness is false. Each object is composed of and contains all others. In the light of the meditation on interdependence, the concept of "one/many" collapses, and takes with it "large/small," "inside/outside," and all the others. The poet Nguyen Cong Tru, upon realizing this, exclaimed:

> In this world and in the worlds beyond,
> Buddha is incomparable!
> Small is not inside.
> Big is not outside.[3]

The Sun My Heart

Since we now realize that "one is all, all is one" in our bodies, let us go another step and meditate on the presence of the entire universe in ourselves. We know that if our heart stops beating, the flow of our life will stop, and so we cherish our heart very much. Yet we do not often take the time to notice that there are other things, outside of our bodies, that are also essential for our survival. Look at the immense light we call the sun. If it stops shining, the flow of our life will also stop, and so the sun is our second heart, our heart outside of our body. This immense "heart" gives all life on Earth the warmth necessary for existence. Plants live thanks to the sun. Leaves absorb the sun's energy, along with carbon dioxide from the air, to produce food for the tree and the flower. In the oceans, phytoplankton process the sun's energy to produce oxygen and nourishment for marine life. Thanks to plants, we and other animals can live. All of us—people, animals, and plants—"consume" the sun, directly and indirectly. We cannot begin to describe all the effects of the sun, that great heart outside of our body. In fact, our body is not limited to what lies inside the boundary of our skin. Our body is much greater, much more immense. If the layer of air around our Earth disappears even for an instant, "our" life will end. There is no phenomenon in the universe that does not intimately concern us, from a pebble resting at the bottom of the ocean, to the movement of a galaxy millions of light years away. The poet Walt Whitman said, "I believe a leaf of grass is no less than the journey-work of the stars...." These words are not philosophy. They come from the depths of his soul. He said, "I am large, I contain multitudes."[4]

Interbeing and Interpenetration

The meditation that I just suggested might also be called "Interbeing Endlessly Interwoven," that is, meditation on the manifestation of all phenomena as interdependent. This meditation can help free us from the concepts of "unity/diversity," or "one/all." This meditation can dissolve the concept of "me," because the concept of self is built on the opposition of unity and diversity. When we think of a speck of dust, a flower, or a human being, our thinking cannot break loose from the idea of unity, of one, of calculation. We see a line between one and many, between one and not one. In daily life we need this just as a train needs a track. But if we truly realize the interdependent nature of the dust, the flower, and the human being, we see that unity cannot exist without diversity. Unity and diversity interpenetrate each other freely. Unity is diversity. This is the principle of interbeing and interpenetration of the Avatamsaka Sutra.

Interbeing means "this is that," and "that is this." Interpenetration means "this is in that," and "that is in this." When we meditate deeply on interbeing and interpenetration, we see that the idea of "one/many" is only a mental construct which we use to contain reality, much as we use a bucket to hold water. Once we have escaped the confinement of this construct, we are like a train breaking free of its rails to fly freely in space. Just as when we realize that we are standing on a spherical planet which is rotating around its own axis and around the sun, our concepts of above and below disintegrate, so when we realize the interdependent nature of all things, we are freed from the idea of "one/many."

The image of Indra's jeweled net is used in the Avatamsaka Sutra to illustrate the infinite variety of interactions and intersections of all things. The net is woven of an infinite variety of brilliant gems, each with countless facets. Each gem reflects in itself every other gem in the net, and its image is reflected in each other gem. In this vision, each gem contains all the other gems.

We can also use an example from geometry. Imagine a circle with its center point "C." The circle is composed of all the points equidistant from C. The circle is there because all the points are there. If even one point is missing, the circle immediately disappears. It is like a house of cards. Remove one card and all the rest collapse. Each card depends on all the others, and without each one there is no house. The presence of one point of the circle depends on the presence of all the other points. Here too we see that "one is all, all is one." Every point of the circle is of equal importance. Every card in the house of cards is of equal importance. Each is vital to the existence of the whole and therefore to the existence of all the other parts. This is interdependence.

To envision the interwoven nature of relationships, which illustrates the character of interbeing and interpenetration, we can picture a sphere which is composed of all the points on its surface and all the points within its volume. There are a great many points, yet without each of them the sphere does not exist. Now let us imagine connecting each point with all the other points. First we connect point A to each of the other points. Then we connect point B with each of the others, including A, and so on until all the points are connected. As you can see we have woven an extremely dense net intertwining all the points.

The Avatamsaka Sutra says, "The Bodhisattva sees the interdependent nature of all things, sees in one dharma all dharmas, sees in all dharmas one dharma, sees the multiplicity in the one and the one in the multiplicity, sees the one in the immeasurable and the immeasurable in the one. Birth and existence of all dharmas is of a changing nature and thus unreal and cannot touch the enlightened ones." As I mentioned earlier, in contemporary physics there is the "bootstrap" idea, which is very close to the idea of interbeing and interpenetration. "Bootstrap physics" renounces the idea of basic elements of matter. The universe is a network of interdependent phenomena in which each phenomenon is formed by the coordination of all other phenomena. The universe is a dynamic fabric of interdependent events in which none is the fundamental entity. What we call particles are only mutual relationships among the particles themselves.[5]

Someone may ask, "Although I agree that each phenomenon depends on all other phenomena for its birth and existence, where does the all, the complete body which includes all phenomena, come from?" Would you please give him an answer?

Eyes Opening in Samadhi

Meditation is not imitation, but creation. Meditators who only imitate their instructors cannot go far. The same is true of cooking, or anything. A good cook is someone with a creative spirit. You can enter the Meditation on the Interdependence of All Phenomena through many different doors—observing your internal organs: blood, heart, intestines, lungs, liver, kidneys; or thousands of other means, including thoughts, feelings, images, poetry, dreams, or a river, a star, a leaf, and so on.

A good practitioner uses meditation throughout daily life, not wasting a single opportunity, a single event, to see deeply the nature of dependent co-arising. All day long, practice is carried out in perfect concentration. With eyes open or closed, the nature of meditation is no other than samadhi. You can discard the idea that you must close your eyes to look inside and open them to look outside. A thought is no more an inner object than a mountain an outer one. Both are objects of knowledge. Neither is inner or outer. Great concentration is achieved when you are fully present, in profound communion with living reality. At these times the distinction between subject and object disappears and you penetrate living reality with ease, are one with it, because you have set aside all tools for measuring knowledge, knowledge which Buddhism calls *vikalpa*, "erroneous knowledge."

Seeing and Loving Always Go Together

There are times while watching our children play that we think about the future. We know that life is filled with worries, fears, hopes, and disappointments, and we worry for them and anxiously think about the struggles before them. It is at that very moment that we *enter* into our children. It is easy to find our way into them because we know they are of our own blood.

Meditation is the same. As we meditate on the interdependent nature of all things, we can penetrate reality easily, and see the fears, anguish, hopes, and despair of all beings. Watching a green caterpillar on a leaf, we understand the importance of the caterpillar, not just from our self-centered point of view as a human, but from the penetration based on the interdependence of all things. Realizing the preciousness of the life of every being, we dare not deprive the caterpillar of its life. If some day we have to kill a caterpillar, we will feel as if we are killing ourselves, that something of ourselves dies with the caterpillar.

In ancient times, people hunted to feed themselves and their families. They did this in order to live. They did not kill just for amusement. Today some people hunt for pleasure. The interdependence of all beings is not a philosophical game removed from spiritual and practical life. In bringing to light the interdependence of all phenomena, the meditator comes to see that the lives of all beings are one, and he or she is overcome with compassion for all. When you feel this love, you know that your meditation is bearing fruit. Seeing and loving always go together. Seeing and loving are one. Shallow understanding accompanies shallow compassion. Great understanding goes with great compassion.

Heartbreak

Have you ever watched a wildlife show on public television in which predators hunt other animals for food? The tiger hunts a deer, or a snake swallows a frog. These shows are filled with suspense. We hope that the deer will escape the tiger's claws, and the frog will be saved from the snake's fangs. It is painful to watch the tiger tear apart the deer and the frog disappear into the snake's mouth. This kind of program is not invented—it is real life. We long for the well-being of the frog and the deer, but rarely do we consider that the tiger and the snake must also eat in order to live. We humans eat chickens, pigs, shrimp, fish, and cows, and, like the tiger and the snake, even deer and frogs. Yet because it is painful to watch, we take the side of the prey and hope it will escape.

In these situations, as meditators, we must remain very clear. We cannot take either side, because we exist in both. Some people can remain unmoved or even enjoy the sight of a tiger tearing apart its prey, but most of us, feeling its agony, take the side of the victim. If a scene like this were occurring in front of us, we would try to find a way to save the deer and the frog. But we have to be careful not to do this just to avoid our own anguish. We must also feel the pain of the tiger or snake deprived of food, and have compassion for them. All beings have to struggle to survive. The more deeply we penetrate into life, the more we see its miracles and the more we see its heartbreaking and terrifying events. Have you seen the life of a spider?

Have you lived through a war? Have you seen torture, prison, and killing? Have you seen a pirate rape a young girl on the high seas?

Reconciliation Originates in the Heart of Compassion

Millions of people follow sports. If you love to watch soccer, you probably root for one team and identify with them. You watch the games with despair and elation. Perhaps you give a little kick to help the ball along. If you do not take sides, the fun is missing. In wars we pick sides, usually the side which is being threatened. Peace movements are born of this feeling. We get angry, we shout, but rarely do we rise above all this to look at a conflict the way a mother would who is watching her two children fighting. She seeks only their reconciliation. Real efforts for reconciliation must arise from this heart of compassion which arises from meditating on the nature of interbeing and interpenetration of all beings.

In our lives, we may be lucky enough to meet someone whose love extends to animals and plants. We may also know people who, although they themselves live in a safe situation, realize that famine, disease, and oppression are destroying millions of people on Earth and look for ways to help those who suffer. They cannot forget them, even amidst the pressures of their own lives. At least to some extent, these people have realized the interdependent nature of life. They know that the survival of the underdeveloped countries cannot be separated from the survival of the materially wealthy, technically advanced countries. Poverty and oppression bring war. In our times, every war involves all countries. The fate of each country is linked to the fate of all others.

Little Room for Compassion

In a civilization where technology is crucial for success, there is little room for compassion. But when we meditate deeply on life, we come to identify even with ants and caterpillars. If we become farmers, we may fail because we will probably refuse to use insecticides to kill pests. And if we do not have the heart to kill an animal, how can we point a gun at another human being? If we become officials in the Department of Defense, we may encourage people to become conscientious objectors. If we become governors, we may oppose building nuclear power plants in our states, and so we will be ousted from the system. Many of us share these kinds of feelings. We are ill at ease with our society, and in a variety of ways we express our opposition.

David Bohm, a physics professor at the University of London, said, "If we want society to change, a few superficial and individual changes, or changes in the economic system are not enough. A complete change in consciousness is necessary. We don't know yet how this change is to be realized, but I am certain that it is absolutely vital."[6] This change of consciousness, as we have seen, can be achieved by realizing the interdependent nature of reality, a realization that each of us can experience in a unique way. This kind of realization is not the result of any ideology or system of thought, but is the fruit of the direct experience of reality in its multiple relationships. It requires the dropping of habitual thinking which fragments reality, a reality that is actually indissoluble.

Fearless in Life and Death

Continue to practice the meditation on interdependence for a while and you will notice a change in yourself. Your perspective will widen, and you will find that you look at all living beings with compassion. The grudges and hatreds that you thought were impenetrable will begin to erode, and you will find yourself caring for each and every being. Most important, you will no longer be afraid of life and death.

Perhaps you have heard of the physicist Erwin Schrödinger, who discovered wave mechanics. After reflecting on the self, life and death, the universe, and unity and multiplicity, he wrote:

> Thus you can throw yourself flat on the ground, stretched out upon Mother Earth, with the certain conviction that you are one with her and she with you. You are as firmly established, as invulnerable as she, indeed a thousand times firmer and more invulnerable. As surely as she will engulf you tomorrow, so surely will she bring you forth anew to new striving and suffering. And not merely "some day":

now, today, every day she is bringing you forth, not
once but thousands upon thousands of times, just
as every day she engulfs you a thousand times over.
For eternally and always there is only *now*, one and
the same now; the present is the only thing that
has no end.[7]

If a view like Schrödinger's is well rooted in our daily
lives, we will be immovable before life and death.

Past, Present, and Future on the Tip of a Hair

Schrödinger's observation about time encourages us to
take another step in our meditation on interdependence.
Our conceptions of inner and outer, one and many, begin
to fall away when we look at the nature of interbeing and
interpenetration of all things. But these ideas will not
drop away completely as long as we believe that absolute
space and absolute time are necessary for the appearance
of all phenomena. In the early days of the Dharmalaksana
("Meditation on Phenomena") school of Buddhism, space
was viewed as an absolute reality outside the realm of
birth and death. When the Madhyamaka ("Meditation on
Noumena," or essential nature) school began to develop,
time and space were described as false conceptions
of reality which depend on one another for existence.
Since the principle of interbeing and interpenetration in
the Avatamsaka Sutra refuses to accept the concepts of
inner/outer, big/small, one/many as real, it also refuses
the concept of space as an absolute reality. With respect

to time, the conceptual distinction between past, present, and future is also destroyed. The Avatamsaka Sutra says that past and future can be put into the present, present and past into the future, present and future into the past, and finally all eternity into one *ksana*, the shortest possible moment. To summarize, time, like space, is stamped with the seal of interdependence, and one instant contains three times: past, present, and future.

> The past in the present and future
> The future in the present and past
> Three times and several aeons in an instant
> Not long, not short—that is liberation.

> I can penetrate the future
> putting all eternity into one instant.

The Avatamsaka Sutra continues, "Not only does a speck of dust contain in itself 'infinite' space, it also contains 'endless' time; in one ksana we find both 'infinite' time and 'endless' space."[8]

> Past present and future on the tip of a hair
> And innumerable Buddha worlds as well.

Entering the World of Interdependence with the Theory of Relativity

The Avatamsaka Sutra says that time and space contain each other, depend on one another for existence, and are not separable by knowledge. The Relativity Theory of

Albert Einstein, born 2,000 years later, confirms the inseparable relationship of time and space. Time is considered the fourth dimension of the four-dimensional space-time continuum.[9] This theory refutes the hypothesis that space is an absolute and immutable framework inside of which the universe is evolving; the idea of absolute and universal time is simultaneously destroyed. It proclaims that space is simply the positional ordering of relationships of things among themselves in a given reference frame, and time is nothing more than the chronological ordering of events in a given reference frame.

Time, according to the theory, can only be local and not universal. This is why the concept "now" can only be applied to "here" and not to other places in the universe. Likewise, "here" can only be applied to this instant, "now," and not to either past or future. This is because time and space can only exist together. They cannot exist independently of one another. This theory allows us to use scientific discoveries about the relative nature of space and time to break down our ideas based on "infinite" space and "endless" time, such ideas as finite and infinite, inside and outside, before and after. If we look up at the sky and wonder what exists beyond the outermost edge of the universe, we still do not understand relativity and still have not shed the idea of an absolute space that exists independent of things. And if we ask where the universe is heading, it is because we still believe in eternal, universal time. The Theory of Relativity contributes to the progress of both science and philosophy. It is a pity that Einstein did not take this superb spaceship even further on the voyage into the world of reality.

A Raft to Cross the River

With all new scientific discoveries comes the destruction of some old ideas of reality. One merit of the Theory of Relativity is that it overturned the classical ideas of time and space through its elaboration of the space-time continuum. According to the theory, everything has a four-dimensional structure and is located in curved four-dimensional space-time. Dropping the Euclidean three-dimensional straight-line model of the universe, Einstein imagined a universe composed of curved lines in a four-dimensional space-time continuum. In 1917 he proposed this model in which space is seen as a three-dimensional facet of a four-dimensional hyperspace, with time as an axis. If we try to imagine this for a sphere, we will no longer see a sphere; instead we will see a hypercylinder in which each minute is a separate sphere, much like the sequence of separate image frames of a film. Einstein's universe is at the same time finite and infinite, because it is composed of curved space-time lines and not separate straight lines that belong either to time or to space. An ant walking on an orange can always go straight ahead, never reaching the end, because it is walking on a curved path. But the ant stays on the orange; that is its limit. Einstein's model generalized straight lines and reconciled finite and infinite.

Yet if endless time and infinite space are only forms of perception, the curved four-dimensional space-time continuum, although closer to reality, is still just another form of perception. If space cannot be conceived of without the presence of "things," the four dimensions of space-time are no more than mental creations in relation to the ideas of "thing" and "movement." The space-time curve must be thought of as only an idea which replaces those of three-dimensional space, endless time, and straight lines. It must be left behind, the same way we leave behind the raft after we have crossed the river.

The Ability to Abandon and the Capacity to Discover

Reality is transformed by our looking at it, because we enter it with our baggage of concepts. Modern physicists know this. Some of them have readily abandoned concepts that have long formed the basis of science—ideas such as cause and effect, and past, present, and future. But it is not easy to abandon concepts. We think that penetrating reality without arming ourselves with ideas is like going into battle empty-handed. The armor of a scientist is his or her acquired knowledge and system of thought, and it is most difficult to leave that behind. I believe that the scientists with the greatest ability to abandon that "armor" are the ones who have the greatest capacity to make discoveries.

Religious seekers have always been reminded that they must let go of all their concepts in order to directly experience reality, from the concepts of self and other, to those of birth and death, permanence and impermanence, existence and nonexistence. If reality is described as inconceivable, the tool to directly experience reality must be a mind free of all concepts.

4

Cutting the Net of Birth and Death

Mind Creates the Form of Reality

YESTERDAY AFTERNOON, little Thuy surprised her teacher. After lunch, she took a broom and swept the classroom floor without anyone asking her to. No child in the village had ever done that before. Later in the afternoon, after class, Thuy's teacher followed her up the hill to our cottage to tell me about it. I told her that all poor children in my country would have done the same thing. They take care of housework by themselves without being asked by the adults.

Today is a French holiday and Thuy is off from school. She and I took a walk this morning, and together we collected pine cones. She told me that the earth gives birth to pine cones so we can use them to start fires to keep warm in winter, but I told her that pine cones are there to give birth to baby pine trees, not for lighting fires. Rather than being disappointed by my explanation, her eyes got even brighter.

Do you remember our conversation about the concepts of space and time in the Avatamsaka Sutra and in the Theory of Relativity? Once we abandon the concepts of absolute space and absolute time, many related concepts that have long formed our patterns of thinking begin to break down. Bootstrap theorists recognize that all atomic particles, such as electrons, cannot exist independently of one another. They are actually "interconnections" among particles, and these "particles" are in turn "interconnections" among other particles. No particle has an independent nature. This is very close to interdependence, interbeing, and interpenetration.

The Theory of Relativity has had a significant influence on our understanding of nuclear particles. In relativity, mass and energy are the same, just as we discovered that rain can be the subject and the verb of a sentence at the same time. When we know that mass is only a form of energy, we come to the realization that "interconnections" among particles are themselves dynamic realities of four-dimensional space-time. For today's scientists, a nuclear particle, just like "a speck of dust" or "the tip of a hair" in the Avatamsaka Sutra, combines both space and time. These particles can be considered a "speck" of time, just as the shortest possible moment (ksana) in the Avatamsaka Sutra is said to contain not only past, present, and future, but also matter and space. A particle can no longer be thought of as a three-dimensional object (like a marble or a speck of dust) situated in space. It has become more abstract to our minds. Electrons, for example, can be called "dynamic four-dimensional bodies in space-time" or "waves of probability." We must keep in mind that words such as "particle," "body," and "wave" no longer have the same meanings as in ordinary language. Contemporary physics has struggled to go beyond the world of concepts, and as a result, particles are now regarded as abstract mathematical quantities (from the point of view of ordinary, discriminative knowledge).

Some scientists proclaim that the properties of nuclear particles are nothing but creations of their own minds, that in reality particles have no properties independent of the minds of those observing them. This implies that in the world of particles, the mind which perceives reality, in fact creates it.

Observer and Participant

For physicists today, the object of mind and the mind itself cannot be separated. Scientists can no longer observe anything with complete objectivity. Their minds cannot be separated from the object. John Wheeler has suggested that we replace the term "observer" with the term "participant." For there to be an "observer," there must be a strict boundary between subject and object, but with a "participant," the distinction between subject and object blurs and even disappears, and direct experience is possible. This notion of a participant/observer is very close to meditation practice. When we meditate on our body, according to the Satipatthana Sutta we meditate on "the body *in* the body." This means that we do not consider our body as a separate object, independent of our mind which is observing it. Meditation is not measuring or reflecting on the object of the mind, but directly perceiving it. This is called "perception without discrimination" (*nirvikalpajñana*).

The habit of distinguishing the mind from its object is so deeply ingrained in us that only gradually, with meditation, can we eliminate it. The Satipatthana Sutta presents four objects of meditation: the body, feelings, mind, and objects of mind. This kind of meditation was practiced by the disciples of the Buddha during his lifetime. Classifying reality this way is to help our meditation, not to help us in the analysis of these things. In the sutta, all material phenomena are regarded as "objects of mind." Of course we can observe that body, feelings, and even mind can also be categorized as "objects of mind." The fact that all phenomena, including material ones, are considered "objects of mind" in the sutta clearly shows that since the earliest times, Buddhism opposed discriminating between mind and its objects.

Mountains Are Again Mountains, Rivers Are Again Rivers

Elementary-particle physicists, when they return home from a day's work in their laboratories, often have the feeling that ordinary objects, such as a chair or a piece of fruit, have lost the substantiality they seemed to have previously. After entering the world of elementary particles, these scientists cannot find anything essential in the world of matter except their own minds. Alfred Kastler

said, "Matter can only be considered from its two comple-
mentary aspects, which are waves and particles. Objects
or things that had always been thought of as constituents
of nature must be renounced."[1]

Although a chair or an orange may no longer be "matter"
for us, we must still sit on the chair and eat the orange. We
are composed of the same essence as they are, even if it is
just a mathematical formula which we ourselves can con-
trive. Meditators realize that all phenomena interpenetrate
and inter-are with all other phenomena, so in their everyday lives they look at a chair or an orange differently from
most people. When they look at mountains and rivers, they
see that "rivers are no longer rivers and mountains are no
longer mountains." Mountains "have entered" rivers, and
rivers "have entered" mountains (interpenetration). Mountains become rivers, and rivers become mountains (interbeing). However, when they want to go for a swim, they have
to go into the river and not climb the mountain. When they
return to everyday life, "mountains are again mountains,
rivers are again rivers."

Neither Form nor Emptiness

A scientist who realizes the nature of interdependence
among particles is likely to be influenced in the way he
or she perceives reality even in everyday life. Because of
this, some kind of transformation may occur in their spiritual life as well. Meditators who realize the interpenetration and interbeing of things also undergo a change in

themselves. Former concepts of "one's self" and "objects" dissolve and they see themselves in everything and all things in themselves. This transformation is the primary goal of meditation. This is why "awareness of being" is maintained throughout the day and not just during periods of meditation. A meditator is aware when he is walking, standing, lying down, and so forth. There are certainly scientists who also do this, reflecting on their topic of research all day long, through their whole being, even as they eat or bathe.

The notion of inter-origination (*paratantra*) is very close to living reality. It annihilates dualistic concepts, one/many, inside/outside, time/space, mind/matter, and so forth, which the mind uses to confine, divide, and shape reality. The notion of inter-origination can be used not only to destroy habits of cutting up reality, but also to bring about a direct experience of reality. As a tool, however, it should not be considered a form of reality in itself.

Paratantra is the very nature of living reality, the absence of an essential self. Just as a triangle exists only because three lines intersect each another, you cannot say any thing exists in itself. Because they have no independent identity, all phenomena are described as empty (*sunya*). This does not mean that phenomena are absent, only that they are empty of an essential self, of a permanent identity that is independent of other phenomena. In the same way, in bootstrap physics the word "particles" does not mean three-dimensional specks which exist independently of one another.

The word "emptiness" here is different from the everyday term. It transcends the usual concepts of emptiness and form. To be empty is not to be nonexistent. It is to be devoid of a permanent identity. To avoid confusion, Buddhist scholars often use the term "true emptiness" to refer to this kind of emptiness. Zen Master Hue Sinh, who lived in the eleventh century during the Ly dynasty in Vietnam, said that we cannot use the words "empty" and "form" to describe objects because reality is beyond these two concepts:

> Dharmas are the same as non-dharmas,
> neither existing nor not existing.
> He who fully understands this
> realizes that all beings are Buddha.

The Udumbara Flower Is Still Blooming

There is a practice called Meditation on True Emptiness, in which the practitioner lets go of habitual ways of thinking about being and nonbeing by realizing that these concepts were formed by incorrectly perceiving things as independent and permanent. When an apple tree produces flowers, we don't see apples yet, and so we might say, "There are flowers but no apples on this tree." We say this because we do not see the latent presence of the apples in the flowers. Time will gradually reveal the apples.

When we look at a chair, we see the wood, but we fail to observe the tree, the forest, the carpenter, or our own mind. When we meditate on it, we can see the entire universe in all its interwoven and interdependent relations in the chair. The presence of the wood reveals the presence of the tree. The presence of the leaf reveals the presence of the sun. The presence of the apple blossom reveals the presence of the apple. Meditators can see the one in the many, and the many in the one. Even before they see the chair, they can see its presence in the heart of living reality. The chair is not separate. It exists only in its interdependent relations with everything else in the universe. It *is* because all other things *are*. If it *is not*, then all other things *are not* either.

Every time we use the word "chair," or the concept "chair" forms in our mind, reality is severed in half. There is "chair" and there is everything that is "not chair." This kind of separation is both violent and absurd. The sword of conceptualization functions this way because we do not realize that the chair is made entirely from non-chair elements. Since all non-chair elements are present in the chair, how can we separate them? An awakened individual vividly sees the non-chair elements when looking at the chair, and realizes that the chair has no boundaries, no beginning, and no end.

When you were small, you may have played with a kaleidoscope. So many wonderful images are formed by bits of colored glass between two lenses and three mirrors. Each time you move your fingers slightly, a new and equally beautiful image appears. We could say that each image has a beginning and an end, but we know that the true nature of it, lenses and colored glass, does not come into being or end with each new configuration. These thousands or millions of patterns are not subject to the notion of "beginning and end." In the same way, we follow our breathing and meditate on the beginningless and endless nature of ourselves and the world. Doing so, we can see that liberation from birth and death is already within reach.

To deny the existence of a chair is to deny the presence of the whole universe. A chair which exists cannot become nonexistent, even if we chop it up into small pieces or burn it. If we could succeed in destroying one chair, we could destroy the entire universe. The concept of "beginning and end" is closely linked with the concept of "being and nonbeing." For example, from what moment in time can we say that a particular bicycle has come into existence and from what moment is it no longer existent? If we say that it begins to exist the moment the last part is assembled, does that mean we cannot say, "This bicycle needs just one more part," in the previous moment? And when it is broken and cannot be ridden, why do we call it "a broken bicycle"? If we meditate on the moment the bicycle *is* and the moment it *is no longer*, we will notice that the bicycle cannot be placed in the categories "being and nonbeing" or "beginning and end."

Did the Indian poet Rabindranath Tagore exist before his birth or not? Does he exist after his death or has he ceased to exist? If you accept the principle from the Avatamsaka Sutra of "interpenetration" or the principle from bootstrap physics of "interbeing," you cannot say that there has ever been a time when "Tagore *is not*," even the times before his birth or after his death. If Tagore is not, the entire universe cannot be, nor can you or I exist. It is not because of his "birth" that Tagore exists, nor because of his "death" that he does not exist.

Late one afternoon I was standing on Vulture Peak in the Indian state of Bihar when I saw a very beautiful sunset, and suddenly I found that Shakyamuni Buddha was still sitting there:

> The great mendicant of old is still there on
>   Vulture Peak,
> contemplating the ever-splendid sunset.
> Gautama, how strange!
> Who said that the Udumbara flower blooms
>   only once every 3,000 years?

> The sound of the rising tide—
> you cannot help hearing it
> if you have an attentive ear.

I have heard several friends express regret that they did not live at the time of the Buddha. I think that even if they passed him on the street, they would not recognize him. Not only Tagore and Shakyamuni Buddha, but all of us are without beginning and without end. I am here because you are there. If any one of us does not exist, no one else can exist either. Reality cannot be confined by concepts of being, nonbeing, birth, and death. The term "true emptiness" can be used to describe reality and to destroy all ideas that imprison and divide us and which artificially create a reality. Without a mind free from preconceived ideas, we cannot penetrate reality. Scientists are coming to realize that they cannot use ordinary language to describe non-conceptual insights. Scientific language is beginning to have the symbolic nature of poetry. Today such words as "charm" and "color" are being used to describe properties of particles that have no conceptual counterpart in the "macro-realm." Some day reality will reveal itself beyond all conceptualizations and measurements.

The Tathagata Neither Arrives nor Departs

This non-conceptualizable reality, or true emptiness, is also called "suchness" (*bhutatathata*). Suchness, sometimes translated "thusness," means "it is so." It cannot be conceived or described through words and concepts but must be directly experienced. Suppose there is a tangerine on the table and someone asks you, "What does it taste like?" Rather than give an answer, you have to section the tangerine and invite the questioner to have a taste. Doing this, you allow him or her to enter the suchness of the tangerine without any verbal or conceptual description.

To remind his disciples of the unconditioned, beginningless and endless nature of reality, Buddha asked them to address him as the Tathagata. This is not an honorific title. Tathagata means "one who thus comes" or "one who thus goes." It means he arises from such-ness, abides in suchness, and returns to suchness, to non-conceptualizable reality. Who or what does not arise from suchness? You and I, a caterpillar, a speck of dust, all arise from suchness, all abide in suchness, and some day will return to suchness. Actually, the words "arise from," "abide in," and "return to" have no real meaning. One can never leave suchness. In the Anuradha Sutta, the Buddha replied to a question that was troubling many monks: "What happens to the Tathagata after death? Does he continue to exist? Does he cease to exist? Does he both continue and cease to exist? Does he neither continue nor cease to exist?"

The Buddha asked Anuradha, "What do you think? Can the Tathagata be recognized through form?"

"No, Master."

"Can you find the Tathagata outside of form?"

"No, Master."

"Can the Tathagata be recognized through feeling, perception, mental formations, or consciousness?"

"No, Master."

"Anuradha, you cannot find the Tathagata even in this life, why do you want to solve the problem of whether I will continue to exist or cease to exist, or both continue and cease to exist, or neither continue nor cease to exist after death?"[2]

Robert Oppenheimer, the physicist known as the father of the first atomic bomb, had a chance to read this section of the Anuradha Sutta. He understood it based on his observations of particles, which cannot be confined by concepts of space, time, being, or not-being. He wrote:

> To what appeared to be the simplest questions, we will tend to give either no answer or an answer which will at first sight be reminiscent more of a strange catechism than of the straightforward affirmatives of physical science. If we ask, for instance, whether the position of the electron remains the same, we must say "no"; if we ask whether the electron's position changes with time, we must say "no"; if we ask whether the electron is at rest, we must say "no"; if we ask whether it is in motion, we must say "no."[3]

As you can see, the language of science has already begun to approach the language of Buddhism. After reading the above quote from the Anuradha Sutta, Oppenheimer said that until this century scientists would not have been able to understand the Buddha's replies of 2,500 years ago.

The Net of Birth and Death Can Be Torn Asunder

There is another meditation which can be used in place of the one on true emptiness. It is called the Meditation on the Miraculousness of Existence. "Existence" means being in the present. "The miraculousness of existence" means to be aware that the universe is contained in each thing, and that the universe could not exist if it did not contain each thing. This awareness of interconnectedness, interpenetration, and interbeing makes it impossible for us to say something "is" or "is not," so we call it "miraculous existence."

Even though Oppenheimer replied "No," four times to the questions about the nature of electrons, he did not mean that electrons are nonexistent. Even though the Buddha said, "You cannot find the Tathagata even in this life," he did not mean that the Tathagata is nonexistent. The Great Prajñaparamita Sutra uses the word "not-empty" (*asunya*) to describe this state. "Not-empty" is the same as "the miraculousness of existence." "True emptiness" and "the miraculousness of existence" can keep us from falling into the trap of discriminating between being and nonbeing.

Both electrons and Tathagata are beyond the concepts of being and nonbeing. The nature of true emptiness and the miraculousness of existence of the electrons and the Tathagata save us from the traps of being and nonbeing and lead us directly into the world of non-conceptualization. How can we practice the meditation on the miraculousness of existence? Anyone who understands the theory of relativity knows that space is intimately connected with both time and matter. For such persons, space has a larger meaning than for persons who still believe that space exists independently of time and matter. When we look at a bee, we may like to see it first through the eyes of a physicist who understands relativity, and then go even beyond that to see true emptiness and the miraculousness of existence in it. If you attempt to do this regularly, with your whole being, I am sure that it will free you from entanglement in the net of birth and death. In Zen circles, the problem of birth and death has always been regarded as the most urgent. Zen Master Hakuin calligraphed the character for Death quite large and then added in smaller strokes: "Anyone who sees to the depths of this word is a true hero."[4]

I used to think that liberation from birth and death was a remote goal. While I was teaching at the Van Hanh Buddhist University in Saigon, I looked at the statues of emaciated Arahats, and I thought it must be necessary to deplete our strength that much, to reduce our desires until total exhaustion overtakes us, to realize this liberation. But later, while I was practicing at Phuong Boi, in central Vietnam, I realized that liberation from birth and death is not an abstract or long-term project. Birth and death are only concepts. To be free from these concepts is to be free from birth and death. It is attainable.

But liberation from birth and death cannot come from intellectual comprehension alone. When you see the interdependent nature of everything in the universe, when you understand the meaning of true emptiness and the miraculousness of existence, you have sown the seeds of liberation in the field of your consciousness. For these seeds to grow we need to practice meditation. Through the practice of meditation, we may become strong enough to break through the concept of birth and death, which is really just one of the many, many concepts we create.

A physicist who is able to see the interpenetration and interbeing of elementary particles without going beyond his or her intellect has, from the viewpoint of Buddhist liberation, attained just a decorative facade. Someone who studies Buddhism without practicing meditation has also accumulated knowledge only as decoration. We hold our own fate in our own hands. We have the capacity to practice until all concepts about birth and death, and being and nonbeing, are uprooted.

The images which I have offered—the sun, an orange, a chair, a caterpillar, a bicycle, electrons, and so forth—can be objects which bring us to a direct experience of reality. Meditate on the sun as your second heart, the heart of your "outer-self." Meditate on the sun in every cell of your body. Meditate to see the sun in plants, in each nourishing morsel of the vegetables you eat. Gradually you will see "the body of ultimate reality" (*dharmakaya*) and recognize your own "true nature." Then birth and death can no longer touch you, and you will have attained success. Tue Trung, a fourteenth-century Vietnamese Zen master, wrote:

> Birth and death,
> you have been crushing me.
> Now you can no longer touch me.

Please meditate deeply on these two sentences until you can notice Tue Trung in each cell of your body.

A Leaf Can Lead Us Directly into Non-Conceptual Reality

The Linji school of Zen in China developed the use of kung-ans (Japanese: *koans*) as tools for awakening. By making the meditator keep one subject in mind, kung-ans aid in creating strong concentration. Here are a few examples of kung-ans that are presented as questions:

> What was your true face before your parents
> brought you into the world?
> What is the sound of one hand clapping?
> Everything returns to the one; where does
> the one return?

Using the form of questions demands our attention. Some kung-ans, such as the following, are not presented as questions, but still have the same questioning effect:

> A dog does not have the nature of awakening.
> Nothing is sacred.
> Te-shan's hair is white, Tche-hai's is black.

Questioning, therefore, is an important element in the practice of meditation using a kung-an. The goal of kung-an practice is to shatter concepts and conceptualizing. Although not their intention, kung-ans sometimes confine the meditator in his or her thoughts and conceptualizations for too long. Often it is only when the practitioner arrives at an impasse and is completely exhausted from conceptual thinking that he or she is ready to drop concepts and return to themself. I think this is a weakness of Zen kung-an practice.

In the meditation on "interbeing" or on "the miraculousness of existence," a practitioner can take any phenomenon as the object of meditation, but she must be able to maintain this for some time, in mindfulness. She may choose the sun, a leaf, a caterpillar. Such meditation is not so enigmatic as kung-an meditation, but if the practitioner is determined to keep the sunlight of their awareness on it hour after hour, they will succeed. This kind of meditation keeps the practitioner from wasting a lot of time straining their intellect looking for solutions to questions that cannot be solved through the intellect. The sun, a leaf, or a caterpillar can take the practitioner directly into the world of non-conceptual reality—a living, direct experience.

Unobstructed Mind and Unobstructed Object

Another important meditation, called "Mind and Object Contain One Another," aims at ending all discrimination between the mind and its objects. When we look at the blue sky, the white clouds, and the sea, we are prone to seeing them as three separate phenomena. But if we look more carefully, we can see that the three are of the same nature and cannot exist independently of one another. If you say, "I was afraid of the snake I just encountered," you treat the snake as physical and fear as psychological. The meditation on Mind and Object Contain One Another is a means of overcoming that kind of separation.

Leibniz, a German mathematician, proposed that not only colors, light, and temperature, but also forms, content, and movement of everything in the universe may be nothing but properties which the mind projects onto reality. In light of quantum theory, no one today can continue to think, as Descartes did, that mind and object are two distinct realities that exist independently and separately from one another.

To say it simply, in the sentence, "I was afraid of the snake," we recognize an "I," a snake, and fear. Fear, a psychological phenomenon, is not only inextricably tied to the physical phenomena "I" and snake, it is inextricably woven into the web of the entire universe and has the same nature as the universe. The concept "fear" includes the concept "snake" and the concept of the person who is afraid of being bitten by the snake. If we try to be objective, we may find ourselves unsure about what exactly is the nature of a snake or the nature of a person, but fear is a direct experience we can recognize and identify.

In the meditation on interdependence, we can see that each moment of consciousness includes the whole universe. This moment might be a memory, a perception, a feeling, a hope. From the point of view of space, we can call it a "particle" of consciousness. From the point of view of time, we can call it a "speck" of time (ksana). An instant of consciousness embraces all past, present, and future, and the entire universe.

When we speak of mind, we usually think of psychological phenomena, such as feelings, thoughts, or perceptions. When we speak of objects of mind, we think of physical phenomena, such as mountains, trees, or animals. Speaking this way, we see the phenomenal aspects of mind and its objects, but we don't see their nature. We have observed that these two kinds of phenomena, mind and objects of mind, rely on one another for their existence and are therefore interdependent. But we do not see that they themselves have the same nature. This nature is sometimes called "mind" and sometimes called "suchness" (*tathata*) or God. Whatever we call it, we cannot measure this nature using concepts. It is boundless and all-inclusive, without limitations or obstacles. From the point of view of unity, it is called "Dharmakaya." From the point of view of duality, it is called "mind without obstacle" encountering "world without obstacle." The Avatamsaka Sutra calls it unobstructed mind and unobstructed object. The mind and the world contain each other so completely and perfectly that we call this "perfect unity of mind and object."

The Great and Perfect Mirror

In 1956, in a lecture on Mind and Matter at Trinity College in Cambridge, the physicist Erwin Schrödinger asked whether consciousness should be singular or plural. He concluded that from the outside, there seem to be many minds but that in reality there is only one.[5] Schrödinger had been influenced by Vedanta philosophy. He was very interested in what he called "the arithmetical paradox" of mind. As we have seen, the separation of one and many is a measurement made by perception. As long as we are prisoners of that separation, we are prisoners of the arithmetical paradox. We can only be free when we see the interbeing and interpenetration of everything. Reality is neither one nor many.

The Vijñanavadins described "perfect unity of mind and object" as "a mirror in which all phenomena are reflected." Without phenomena, there can be no reflections, and without reflections, there can be no mirror. The image used to describe mind is "a large, round mirror which nothing can cover and nothing can hide." All phenomena are said to be stored in a "storehouse" (*alaya*). The contents and the proprietor (subject of knowledge) in this store are one. In the teachings of the Vijñanavadins, alaya contains the seeds (*bija*) of all physical, physiological, and psychological phenomena. At the same time it functions as the ground from which the subjects and objects of knowledge arise. Alaya is not bounded by space or limited by time. In fact, even space and time arise from alaya.[6]

Crucial to the Vijñanavada teaching is understanding the object of perception. They are of three types: pure objects or reality in itself (*svabhava*), representations or conceptualized visible objects (*samanya laksana*), and pure images or conceptualized objects that remain in memory and may reappear in the mind when the correct conditions are present.

Manyana and Vijñapti

From the alaya arise two kinds of consciousness, *manyana* and *vijñapti*. Vijñapti causes all feelings, perceptions, concepts, and thoughts to appear. It is based in the sense organs, the nervous system, and the brain. The object of vijñapti is reality in itself (svabhava) which is possible only when feelings and perceptions are pure and direct. When seen through the veil of conceptualization, the same object can be only an image of reality (samanya lak-sana) or a pure image such as a dream while asleep or a daydream. Although the object of a pure sensation is reality in itself, when this reality is seen through concepts and thoughts, it is already distorted. Reality in itself is a stream of life, always moving. Images of reality produced by concepts are concrete structures framed by the concepts of space/time, birth/death, production/destruction, existence/nonexistence, one/many.

Manyana is a kind of intuition, the sense that there is a separate self that can exist independently of the rest of the world. This intuition is produced by habit and ignorance. Its illusory nature has been constructed by vijñapti, and it, in turn, becomes a basis for vijñapti. The object of this intuition is a distorted fragment of alaya which it considers to be a self, comprised of a body and a soul. It, of course, is never reality in itself, but just a representation of reality. In its role as a self as well as consciousness of the self, manyana is regarded as the basic obstacle to penetrating reality. Contemplation performed by vijñapti can remove the erroneous perceptions brought about by manyana.

Within vijñapti, there are six consciousnesses: consciousness of seeing, hearing, smelling, tasting, touching, and thinking. The mind consciousness (*manovijñana*) has the broadest field of activity. It can be active in conjunction with the other senses, for example, awareness of seeing. It can also be active on its own, such as in conceptualizing, reflecting, imagining, and dreaming. Following the five consciousnesses of the senses, mind consciousness is called the sixth consciousness. Manyana, or *manas*, and alaya are the seventh and eighth consciousnesses.

To See Reality with the Eyes of Understanding

As already mentioned, it is only in the case of pure sensation that the object of consciousness is reality-in-itself. The senses are only of relative value in penetrating reality. That is why, although the content of any sensation is reality-in-itself, what is sensed is never reality in its entirety. Science has shown, for example, that human eyes can perceive only a minute portion of the electromagnetic spectrum. Radio waves are invisible to us because their frequencies are too low for us to see. When we see light and hear sounds, we perceive only waves within certain frequencies. Infrared rays are invisible to us, as they have longer wavelengths than are visible to us. Since X-rays have shorter wavelengths than those of visible light, we cannot see them either. Everything in the universe would appear quite different if we could see X-rays! Nor can we hear the high-pitched sounds to which the ears of dogs and other animals are sensitive. Among animals on the Earth, many can perceive much more of reality than we humans can.

Therefore, the perfect ultimate reality of the universe can only be observed with eyes of great understanding, but these eyes can only open when the concepts that compose the manyana and attachment to wrong views are uprooted. Only then can the alaya reveal itself as a great, perfect mirror reflecting the whole universe.

Is Alaya One or Many?

If we were to ask, "Does everyone have his or her own alaya, or do we all share a common alaya?" it would show that we have not yet realized the true nature of interbeing and interpenetration. We are still bewildered by what Schrödinger called the "arithmetical paradox." We may then ask, "If we do not each have separate alayas, why do we have separate, individual memories?"

Can we say that one child learns his lesson and another knows it by heart? Waves break on the water's surface, and although they cannot exist apart from the water, they have their own form and their own place. Many streams may flow into a river, but all of them are one with the river. On the surface of the sea of phenomena, we see many waves glistening, but for each wave to be formed, for each to be destroyed, it must be dependent on every other wave. The memories of each of us are not just our own personal treasures. They are living realities that are related to all other living realities. They undergo ceaseless transformation, as do our bodies. Each thing is reality, but reality is not subject to ideas of "one" or "many."

Let the Sun of Awareness Shine on the Dharmakaya

These teachings from the Vijñanavada school are given to us to help our meditation practice, not as descriptions of reality. We should not forget that the phenomena that we call the sixth and seventh consciousnesses, reality-in-itself, or representations of reality, do not exist independently of one another or of space-time. A representation of an object that appears in a dream is also a living reality in which the whole universe is present. We often think that an image of a fairy in a dream has no reality since it is without material basis, but what about the images on our TV screens? Are they real? Can we grasp their substance or find their material basis? Still, they are real. The entire universe is present in them. The presence of an illusion includes everything in the universe. The illusion can exist only because everything else exists. Its existence has the same marvelous nature as a particle. In modern science, a particle is no longer seen as solid or concretely defined.

When the sixth *vijñana*, mind consciousness, remains in deep concentration, it does not create illusory objects. At such times, a living and direct experience of ultimate reality is possible. To be conscious always means to be conscious of something. Therefore we should not think that we can bring our consciousness to a "pure" state in which there are no objects. A consciousness without an object is a consciousness that is not manifested. It is latent in the alaya, just as a wave is latent in calm water. There is a state of concentration which can be attained during meditation, called "concentration without perception," in which consciousness is no longer active. In dreamless sleep, consciousness also remains in this latent state in the alaya.

During meditation, we focus all our attention on one object, and concentration can arise. This meditation is not passive or dull; in fact we must be very alert. We maintain concentration on the object, which is the mind itself, just as the sun continues to shine on freshly fallen snow or vegetation. We can also synchronize our breathing with our attention to the object, and this may improve our concentration. If we use a leaf as the object of our concentration, we can see, through the leaf, the perfect oneness of mind and universe. If we meditate on the presence of the sun throughout our body, we can experience that Dharmakaya has no beginning and no end. Meditating on interbeing and interpenetration of reality is a means to destroy concepts, and using such means, we can arrive at a direct experience of ultimate reality in mind and body simultaneously. In the Vijñanavada school, this is called *vijñaptimatrata*.

From Interdependence (Paratantra) to Perfect Reality (Nispañña)

The practice of meditation on the three-fold nature of things (*tri-svabhava*) is similar to meditation on the principle of multi–inter-origin. In both cases, we begin by meditating on the interdependent relationship of all things (paratantra) in order to realize that the image of reality we have in our mind is erroneous because it is built within the framework of birth/death, one/many, space/time, and other concepts, i.e., it is based on illusion. By looking deeply into reality in the light of interdependence, we gradually free ourselves from the net of clinging to "myself" as a separate self and all dharmas as separate "own-beings." Even if in the alaya many deep roots of illusion (*anusaya*) still exist, they can be uprooted and destroyed, and perfect liberation achieved each moment that is fully lived in the light of interdependence. Just as the raft is no longer needed after we reach the other shore, when we live in the present moment in harmony with all beings, we do not need the concept of interdependence. We can dwell peacefully in the true nature of consciousness. This is called ultimate reality. It is the world of suchness (tathata), the world of perfect oneness of mind and object.

Conditioned Reality and Ultimate Reality Cannot Be Separated

There is no need for us to attain the world of suchness, because suchness is available at all times. The Avatamsaka Sutra calls it the "Dharma Realm of Truth," the world of true nature. The world of mountains and rivers, plants and animals, where each thing seems to have its own place, is called the "Dharma Realm of Phenomena." But these two worlds are not separate. They are one, exactly like water and waves. That is why they are also referred to as the "Dharma Realm of Unobstructed Interpenetration of Truth and Phenomena." Interpenetration in this world of phenomena, where one phenomenon is all phenomena and where all are one is called the "Dharma Realm of Unobstructed Interpenetration of Every Phenomenon." These are called the Four Dharma Realms, mentioned frequently in the Avatamsaka Sutra. Zen Master Fa Cang of Tang dynasty China, one of the great scholars in this field, wrote a text that describes the methods of meditation that can help us destroy wrong views and return to the source, prior to their origination, which means having a clear, perfect view of the world of suchness.[7]

David Bohm has expounded a theory on what he calls "the implicate order and the explicate order," which is very close to the notion of the Dharma Realm of the Unobstructed Interpenetration of All Phenomena. Bohm has said that all realities which are thought to exist independently of one another belong to the explicate order, an order in which one thing seems to exist outside of another. However, if we see deeply, everything is linked to everything else in the whole universe, and from one particle we can see the whole universe, which is included in it and out of which it is created. This leads us to the world of the implicate order in which "time and space no longer decide whether things are dependent on or independent of one another." According to Bohm, present-day science must start from the wholeness of the implicate order to be able to see the real nature of each phenomenon. At the conference in Córdoba, he said, "The electron is always the whole."[8] This view is very close to the "one in the all" of the Avatamsaka Sutra. If scientists like Bohm are willing to go even further in their research and practice meditation, which involves both mind and body, they may well arrive at some unexpected result and cause a major breakthrough in physics.

Look Deeply at Your Hand

Happiness Arises from Awareness of Being

THE SKY WAS CLEAR and it was quite warm this morning. Little Thuy left for school after eating the fried rice I made for her, and I went into the garden to transplant some lettuce. When I came in to wash my hands, I saw that my guest was already awake and washing his face. I boiled water and made a pot of tea. With two cups on the table in the courtyard, I sat and waited for him to come outside.

We drank tea in the warm sunshine. My friend asked me how we can see the results of meditation, and I told him that peace and happiness are the guides for measuring the fruit of practice. If we do not become calmer and happier, something is wrong with our practice.

Sometimes people say that without a teacher, meditation can cause confusion and imbalance, but it is not always possible to find a highly developed teacher. Such people are rare, although it is often possible to find teachers who have not yet fully realized the Way. If you are not able to study with a realized teacher, the most intelligent way to practice is to rely primarily on the teacher in yourself.

Proceed slowly and carefully. For example, it is not necessary to practice the Four Formless Meditations.

Never force your body or your mind. Be kind to yourself. Live your daily life simply, with awareness. If you are mindful, you have everything; you are everything! Please have a look at *The Miracle of Mindfulness* and The Sutra on the Full Awareness of Breathing.[1] They are filled with practical suggestions concerning the practice. Read the sections on the Four Dharma Realms, the Eight Consciousnesses, and the Three Natures. Reading books with practical suggestions is useful, not just before practicing sitting meditation but anytime. A minute of meditation is a minute of peace and happiness. If meditation is not pleasant for you, you are not practicing correctly.

Meditation brings happiness. This happiness comes, first of all, from the fact that you are master of yourself, no longer caught up in forgetfulness. If you follow your breathing and allow a half-smile to blossom, mindful of your feelings and thoughts, the movements of your body will naturally become more gentle and relaxed, harmony will be there, and true happiness will arise. Keeping our mind present in each moment is the foundation of meditation practice. When we achieve this, we live our lives fully and deeply, seeing things that others, in forgetfulness, do not.

Providing Conditions Conducive to Living in Mindfulness

In *The Miracle of Mindfulness*, I proposed more than thirty exercises of mindfulness, including a suggestion for how to arrange one day of mindfulness each week. If you read it, you will see clear instructions. This book has been translated into thirty-five languages. It is a small book, but it is very practical and easy to read. In fact, I still follow its instruction myself. You can read it many times, because each time you read it you will have a chance to examine your own practice and from your own experience discover things not in the book. Decades have passed since it was published, and I still receive many letters from readers all over the world expressing their gratitude, telling how this book has brought great changes in their lives. A surgeon in New York told me that he always maintains mindfulness while performing operations. (I think to myself that this surgeon will never forget his surgical instruments in his patients' bodies.)

The first few months of your practice may lack continuity, since it is natural to forget to practice mindfulness sometimes. But you can always start again. If you have a practicing companion, you are very lucky. Friends who practice together often remind each other to practice mindfulness, and they can share experiences and progress. Mindfulness can be nurtured in you by many different means. An autumn leaf that you pick up in your backyard can be taped to your bathroom mirror, and every morning when you see it, the leaf will remind you to smile and return to mindfulness. While you wash your face and brush your teeth, you will be relaxed and in mindfulness. A bell from a nearby church or clock tower, or even the telephone can also bring you back to mindfulness. I recommend you let the phone ring two or three times before answering, while you breathe in and out and take the time to return to your true self.

My Love, Who Are You?

Some day, if you need a topic for meditation, choose one that you care about, one that you find very interesting, so that it will command your attention. It can be the sun, a caterpillar, a dewdrop, time, your face and your eyes before you were born. Every phenomenon, concrete or abstract, physical, physiological, psychological, or meta-physical, can be the subject of your meditation. After you choose a topic, plant it in the depths of your spiritual life. An egg needs to be incubated by its mother hen in order to become a baby chick. In the same way, the topic you sow must be nurtured. Your "self," or the "self" of the person you like the most, or the "self" of the person you hate the most can be the subject of your practice. Any sub-ject can bring about awakening if it is sown deeply into the ground of your being. But if it is only entrusted to your intellect, it is unlikely to bear fruit.

Have you meditated on the subject "Who am I?" Who were you before you were born? At the time when there was not the slightest trace of your physical existence, did you exist or not? How can you become something from nothing? If on the day I was conceived my parents had had other appointments and had not been able to see each other, then who would I be now? If that day the egg of my mother had not been penetrated by that sperm of my father, but by another sperm of his, then who would I be now? Would I be a brother or a sister of mine? If that day, my mother had not married my father or my father had not married my mother, but had married someone else, then who would I be today?" Each healthy living cell in your body controls its own activity, but does this mean that each cell has its own self? In the biological classification system, species make up smaller subdivisions of genus. Does each species represent a "self"? If such questions are asked with your deepest conviction and intelligence, and if you plant them deeply into your spiritual life with your whole being, one day an unexpected discovery will arise.

Have you ever looked into the eyes of your loved one and asked deeply, "Who are you, my love?" For either of you to answer, you cannot be satisfied by the usual responses. "My love, who are you who comes to me and takes my suffering as your suffering, my happiness as your happiness, my life and death as your life and death? Who are you whose 'self' has become my 'self'? My love, why aren't you a dewdrop, a butterfly, a bird, a pine tree?" Don't be satisfied with mere poetic images. You must ask and answer these questions with your whole mind and heart, with your whole being. Someday, you will even have to question the person you hate the most in this same way: "Who are you who brings me such pain, who makes me feel so much anger and hatred? Are you part of the chain of cause and effect, the fire which forges me on the path?" In other words, "Are you me myself?" You have to become that person. You have to be one with him or her, to worry about what he or she worries about, to suffer his or her suffering, to appreciate what he or she appreciates. That person and you cannot be "two." Your "self" cannot be separate from their self. You are that person, the same as you are your love, and the same as you are yourself.

Continue practicing until you see yourself in the most cruel and inhumane political leader, in the most devastatingly tortured prisoner, in the wealthiest man, and in the child starving, all skin and bones. Practice until you recognize your presence in everyone else on the bus, in the subway, in the concentration camp, working in the fields, in a leaf, in a caterpillar, in a dewdrop, in a ray of sunshine. Meditate until you see yourself in a speck of dust and in the most distant galaxy.

Standard for Orientation

As you continue practicing, the flower of insight will blossom in you, along with the flowers of compassion, tolerance, happiness, and letting go. You can let go, because you do not need to keep anything for yourself. You are no longer a fragile and small "self" that needs to be preserved by all possible means. Since the happiness of others is also your happiness, you are now filled with joy, and you have no jealousy or selfishness. Free from attachment to wrong views and prejudices, you are filled with tolerance. The door of your compassion is wide open, and you also suffer the sufferings of all living beings. As a result, you do whatever you can to relieve these sufferings. These four virtues are called the Four Immeasurable Minds: loving kindness, compassion, sympathetic joy, and inclusiveness. They are the fruits of the meditation on the principle of the interdependent co-arising of things. The development of these Four Immeasurable Minds in you shows that you are proceeding in the right direction and are also capable of guiding others in their practice.

A Love Letter

Where are you now, my good friend? Are you out in the field, in the forest, on the mountain, in a military camp, in a factory, at your desk, in a hospital, in prison? Regardless of where you are, let us breathe in and out together, and let the Sun of Awareness enter. Let us begin with this breath and this awareness. Whether life is an illusion, a dream, or a wondrous reality depends on our insight and our mindfulness. Awakening is a miracle. The darkness in a totally dark room will disappear the moment the light is switched on. In the same way, life will reveal itself as a miraculous reality the second the Sun of Awareness begins to shine.

I have a poet friend who was put into a "reeducation" camp in Vietnam, in a remote jungle area. During his four . years there, he practiced meditation and was able to live in peace. Upon release, he was lucid, like a sharp sword. He knew that he had not lost anything during those four years. On the contrary, he knew he had "reeducated himself in meditation."

As I write these lines, I am writing a love letter. I hope these words will be read by you, my known and unknown brothers and sisters, who are living in circumstances regarded as hopeless and tragic, that you may renew your energies and courage.

If You Want Peace, Peace Is with You Immediately

In the early 1970s, I wrote four Chinese characters on a paper lampshade. These four characters can be translated as, "If you want peace, peace is with you immediately." A few years later, in Singapore, I had the chance to practice these words.

Several of us organized a program to help the Indochinese refugees in the Gulf of Siam. The program was called *Mau Chay Ruot Mem* ("When blood is shed, we all suffer"). At that time, the world did not know about the "boat people," and the governments of Thailand, Malaysia, and Singapore would not allow them to land. So we hired two large ships, the Leapdal and the Roland, to pick up refugees on the open sea, and two small ships, the Saigon 200 and the Blackmark, to communicate between them and to transport food and supplies. We planned to fill the two large ships with refugees and take them to Australia and Guam. We had to do our work secretly, since the situation of the boat people was something most of the world's governments did not want to acknowledge at that time, and we knew they would give us a hard time if they found out.

Unfortunately, after nearly eight hundred refugees had been rescued from small boats at sea, the government of Singapore discovered our program. At two o'clock one morning, the Singapore police were ordered to surround the house where I was staying. One officer blocked the front and another the back, while four others rushed in and confiscated my travel documents. They ordered me to leave the country within twenty-four hours.

With eight hundred people aboard our two large ships, we had to find a way for them to travel safely to Australia or Guam. The Saigon 200 and the Blackmark were not allowed to leave port to take food and water to the refugees on the Leapdal and the Roland. The Roland had enough fuel to reach Australia if we could get food to them. Then its engine broke down. The day was very windy and the sea quite rough, and we worried about the ship's safety, even drifting offshore, but the Malaysian government would not allow it to enter Malaysian waters. I tried to get permission to enter a neighboring country, to continue the rescue operation, but the governments of Thailand, Malaysia, and Indonesia would not grant me an entry visa. Even though I was on land, I found myself drifting on the sea and my life was one with the lives of the eight hundred refugees on board.

In that situation, I decided that I must practice the meditation topic: "If you want peace, peace is with you immediately," and I was surprised to find myself quite calm, not afraid or worried about anything. I was not just careless—this was truly a peaceful state of mind. And in that state of mind, I was able to overcome this difficult situation. As long as I live, I will never forget those seconds of sitting meditation, those breaths, those mindful footsteps during that twenty-four-hour period.

There were more problems than it seemed possible to solve in just twenty-four hours. Even in a whole lifetime, many of us complain that there is not enough time. How could so much be done in a mere twenty-four hours? Success came when I faced the problem directly. I vowed that if I could not have peace at that moment, I would never be able to have peace. If I could not be peaceful in the midst of danger, then the kind of peace I might have in simpler times would not mean anything. Without finding peace in the midst of difficulty, I would never know real peace. Practicing this topic, "If you want peace, peace is with you immediately," I was able to resolve many problems, one after another, when that was what was needed.

Effect Follows Cause More Quickly than a Bolt of Lightning

Peace can exist only in the present moment. It is ridiculous to say, "Wait until I finish this, then I will be free to live in peace." What is "this"? A diploma, a job, a house, the payment of a debt? If you think that way, peace will never come. There is always another "this" that will follow the present one. If you are not living in peace at this moment, you will never be able to. If you truly want to be at peace, you must be at peace right now. Otherwise, there is only "the hope of peace someday."

My poet-friend did not wait to be released from the reeducation camp to live in peace. He did not know that he would only be there four years. (Many stay ten years or longer.) He practiced meditation on a topic similar to, "If you want peace, peace is with you immediately." We need to sit down and find a method of practice that works for us so we can live in peace and happiness. Peace does not come only after many long days of practice. What is most important is your wish, your determination. If your determination is strong, the effect will follow the cause more quickly than a bolt of lightning. You can nurture peace through your breathing, your footsteps, or your smile, through seeing, hearing, or feeling, until you are one with peace.

Everything Depends on Your Peace

If the earth were your body, you could feel the many areas where there is suffering. War, suppression, and famine wreak destruction in so many places. Many children have become blind from malnutrition. Their hands search through mounds of trash for things they can trade for a few ounces of food. Many adults are dying slowly and hopelessly in prisons. Others are killed for trying to oppose the violence. We have enough nuclear weapons to destroy dozens of Earths, but we continue to manufacture more.

Aware of all of this, how can we withdraw to a forest or even to our own room to sit in meditation? The peace we seek cannot be our personal possession. We need to find an inner peace which makes it possible for us to become one with those who suffer, and to do something to help our brothers and sisters, which is to say, ourselves. I know many young people who are aware of the real situation of the world and who are filled with compassion. They refuse to hide themselves in artificial peace, and they engage in the world in order to change society. They know what they want, yet after a period of involvement they become discouraged. Why? It is because they lack deep, inner peace, the kind of peace they can take with them into their life of action. Our strength is not in weapons, money, or power. Our strength is in our peace, the peace within us. This peace makes us indestructible. We must have peace while taking care of those we love and those we want to protect.

I have recognized this peace in many, many people. Most of their time and effort is spent protecting the weak, watering the trees of love and understanding everywhere. They belong to various religious and cultural backgrounds. I do not know how each of them came to their inner peace, but I have seen it in them. If you are attentive, I am sure you will see it too. This peace is not a barricade which separates you from the world. On the contrary, this kind of peace brings you into the world and empowers you to undertake whatever you want to do to try to help—struggling for social justice, lessening the disparity between the rich and the poor, stopping the arms race, fighting against discrimination, and sowing more seeds of understanding, reconciliation, and compassion. In any struggle, you need determination and patience. This determination will dissipate if you lack peace. Those who lead a life of social action especially need to practice mindfulness during each moment of daily life.

A Bodhisattva Looks at All Beings with the Eyes of Compassion

Peace and compassion go hand in hand with understanding and nondiscrimination. We choose one thing over another when we discriminate. With the eyes of compassion, we can look at all of living reality at once. A compassionate person sees himself or herself in every being. With the ability to view reality from many viewpoints, we can overcome all viewpoints and act compassionately in each situation. This is the highest meaning of the word "reconciliation."

Reconciliation does not mean to sign an agreement with duplicity and cruelty. Reconciliation opposes all forms of ambition, without taking sides. Most of us want to take sides in each encounter or conflict. We distinguish right from wrong based on partial evidence gathered directly or by propaganda or hearsay. We need indignation in order to act, but indignation alone is not enough, even righteous, legitimate indignation. Our world does not lack people willing to throw themselves into action.

What we need are people who are capable of loving, of not taking sides so that they can embrace the whole of reality as a mother hen embraces all her chicks, with two fully spread wings.

The practice of meditation on interdependent co-arising is one way to arrive at this realization. When it is attained, discrimination vanishes and reality is no longer sliced by the sword of conceptualization. The boundaries between good and evil are obliterated, and means and ends are recognized as the same. We have to continue practicing until we can see a child's body of skin and bones in Uganda or Ethiopia as our own, until the hunger and pain in the bodies of all living species are our own. Then we will have realized nondiscrimination, real love. According to the Lotus Sutra, looking at all living beings with the eyes of compassion is a capacity of Avalokitesvara Bodhisattva.[2] When we see someone who can look at all beings with the eyes of compassion, we know that Avalokitesvara Bodhisattva is present in them. When we meditate on the First Noble Truth, the truth of suffering, Avalokitesvara Bodhisattva is present in us. When we ask a favor of Avalokitesvara Bodhisattva, he appears even before we ask.

Look into Your Hand, My Child

I have a friend who is an artist. He has been away from home for nearly forty years. He told me that every time he misses his mother, all he has to do is look at his hand and he feels better. His mother, a traditional Vietnamese woman, could read only a few Chinese characters and has never studied Western philosophy or science. Before he left Vietnam, she held his hand and told him, "Whenever you miss me, look into your hand, my child. You will see me immediately." How penetrating are these simple, sincere words! For nearly forty years, he has looked into his hand many times.

The presence of his mother is not just genetic. Her spirit, her hopes, and her life are also present in him. I know that my friend practices meditation, but I do not know whether he has chosen the subject "Looking into Your Hand" as a kung-an. This subject can take him far in his practice. From his hand, he can penetrate deeply into the reality of beginningless and endless time. He will be able to see that thousands of generations before him and thousands of generations after him are all him. From time immemorial until the present moment, his life has never been interrupted and his hand is still there, a beginningless and endless reality. He can recognize his "true face" five hundred million years ago and five hundred million years from now. He exists not only in the evolutionary tree branching along the axis of time, but also in the network of interdependent relations. As a result, each cell in his body is just as free from birth and death as he is. In this case, the subject "Looking into Your Hand" can produce a deeper effect than the subject "The Sound of One Hand" proposed by Zen Master Hakuin.

When my niece came to visit me from America last summer, I gave her "Looking into Your Hand" as a Zen subject for her to cherish. I told her that every pebble, every leaf, every caterpillar on the hill by the hermitage is present in her hand.

Why Do You Cry, Sister?

Some years ago, a pro-government group in Ho Chi Minh City spread a rumor that I had passed away from a heart attack. This news caused much confusion inside the country.

A Buddhist nun wrote me that the news arrived at her community while she was teaching a class of novices, and the atmosphere in the class sank and one nun passed out. I had already been in exile for about twenty years because of my involvement in the peace movement, and I did not know this young nun or her generation of Buddhist monks and nuns in Vietnam.[3] But life and death is only a fiction, and not very deep; why do you cry, sister? You are studying Buddhism, doing what I am doing. So if you exist, I also exist. What does not exist cannot come into existence and what exists cannot cease to be. Have you realized that, sister? If we cannot bring a speck of dust from "existence" to "nonexistence," how can we do that to a human? On Earth, many people have been killed struggling for peace, for human rights, for freedom and social justice, but no one can destroy them. They still exist. Sister, do you think that Jesus Christ, Mahatma Gandhi, Grigoris Lambrakis, Dr. Martin Luther King Jr. are dead people? No, they are still here. We are they. We carry them in each cell of our bodies. If you ever hear such news again, please smile. Your serene smile will prove that you have attained great understanding and courage. Buddhism and all of humankind expect this of you.

All Is in the Word "Know"

A friend of mine who is a research scientist is now guiding many PhD candidates on their theses. He wants to do everything in a scientific way, but he is also a poet and as a result he often is not very "scientific." Last winter, he went through a tremendous spiritual crisis. Hearing of this, I sent him a drawing of a wave riding on silky-smooth water. Beneath the drawing I wrote, "As always, the wave lives the life of a wave, and at the same time, the life of water. When you breathe, you breathe for all of us."

As I wrote that sentence, I swam with him to help him get across that time of difficulty, and fortunately, it helped us both. Most people view themselves as waves and forget that they are also water. They are used to living in birth-and-death, and they forget about no-birth and no-death. A wave also lives the life of water, and we also live the life of no-birth and no-death. We only need to know that we are living the life of no-birth and no-death. All is in the word "know." To know is to realize. Realization is mind-fulness. All the work of meditation is aimed at awakening us in order to know one and only one thing: birth and death can never touch us in any way whatsoever.

Notes

Chapter One: Sunshine and Green Leaves

1. See also Thich Nhat Hanh, *Understanding Our Mind: 50 Verses on Buddhist Psychology* (Berkeley, CA: Parallax Press, 2006).
2. "In the Forest," from Thich Nhat Hanh, *Call Me By My True Names: The Collected Poems of Thich Nhat Hanh* (Berkeley, CA: Parallax Press, 1999).
3. In the teaching of Vijñanavada, *smrti* is accompanied by *samadhi* and *prajña*, and forgetfulness is accompanied by dispersion and wrong views. Dispersion and wrong views are the opposites of samadhi and prajña. Smrti, samadhi, and prajña are three among the five wholesome mental formations. Forgetfulness, dispersion, and wrong views are three among the twenty-six unwholesome mental formations. .
4. Fritjof Capra, *The Tao of Physics: An Exploration of the Parallels between Modern Physics and Eastern Mysticism* (Boston: Shambhala New Science Library, Second Edition, 1985). See also Thomas Cleary, trans., *The Flower Ornament Scripture: A Translation of the Avatamsaka Sutra*, 3 volumes (Boston: Shambhala, 1984–87)
5 See, e.g., Dogen, *Moon in a Dewdrop*, ed. Kazuaki Tanahashi (Berkeley, CA: North Point Press, 1985), p. 314.
6. Although in the Copenhagen interpretation of quantum theory, observer and observed are inseparable, most scientists do not practice this preaching.
7. Satipatthana Sutta, Majjhima Nikaya MN10; (PTS) M i 55. For the sutra and commentaries, see Thich Nhat Hanh, *Transformation and Healing* (Berkeley, CA: Parallax Press, 2002).
8. "The terms "objective" and "subjective" only designate limited events. Through quantum mechanics we know that no totally objective phenomenon can exist, that is to say, independent of the observer's mind. Correlatively, all subjective phenomena present an objective fact." Brian D. Josephson, *Science et conscience* (Paris: France-Culture/Colloque de Cordoue, 1980).

Chapter Two: The Dance of the Bees

1. See David Bohm, *Wholeness and the Implicate Order* (London: Routledge & Kegan Paul, 1980), Chapter 2, on the "rheomode."
2. Alphonse de Lamartine, *Méditations poétiques* (1820).

3. *Alaya,* the eighth consciousness, has the function of "maintaining" the maintainer, the object that is maintained, and the object taken as a self by the seventh consciousness, *manyana.* Alaya also has the function of maintaining all seeds (*bija*), i.e., transforming and making ripe all karmas so that new physical, psychological, and physiological phenomena arise. Manyana is a psychological attempt to cling to a part of alaya as itself. *Amala* is pure white consciousness—the name of *alaya* after it is freed from manyana. All of this is more fully explained in Chapter Four.

Chapter Three: The Universe in a Speck of Dust

1. Many believe that entering the Four Dhyanas and the Four Formless States Samadhi is to enter a state in which mind no longer has its object. In fact, mind always has an object—if not, it is not mind. In the Four Formless States, the object of the mind is limitless space, limitless consciousness, the absence of perception, and the state of neither perception nor non-perception. Samadhi is a state of mind in which the distinction of subject and object of consciousness no longer exists, i.e., the *nimittabhaga* (object) is not objectivized by the *darsanabhaga* (subject). Both object and subject are parts of consciousness; they cannot exist separately. They have the same ground of being, the *svabhavabhaga* (the self-nature of consciousness).

2. Dao Hanh, Zen master, Ly dynasty, end of the eleventh century.

3. Nguyen Cong Tru was born in 1778 in the Vietnamese village of Uy Vieu, in Ha Tinh province, and he died in 1859.

4. Walt Whitman, "Song of Myself." "Do I contradict myself?/Very well then, I contradict myself/I am large, I contain multitudes."

5. "It is a question here, on the contrary, of pushing to the limit the conception of particles as a network of related interconnections. The philosophy of bootstrap renounces not only the idea of elementary building blocks of matter, but any fundamental entity of any kind: laws, equations, or principles. In it the universe is a dynamic tissue of interdependent events. No property of any part of it has the role of foundation; all is the result of the properties of the other parts, and it is the global coherence of their mutual relationships which determines the structure of the whole tissue." Fritjof Capra, "The Tao of Physics," in Josephson, ed., *Science and Conscience* (Paris, 1980), op. cit.

6. David Bohm, "Imagination and the Implicate Order," in Josephson, op. cit., p. 453.

7. Erwin Schrödinger, *My View of the World* (London: Cambridge University Press, 1964), p. 22.

8. The terms "endless" (*vo ang*) and "infinite" (*vo tan*) are in quotes because I am using them provisionally.

9. Before Einstein, the German mathematician Minkowski had already said that time and space separated from each other are fictitious ghosts; only when together can they represent reality. The Theory of Relativity says that all moving things (all pieces of rock on Earth are moving together with Earth also) can only assert themselves in time and space at the same time. For example, if a plane takes off from Paris to go to New Delhi, the flight controller on the ground not only has to know the longitude, the latitude, and the altitude, but he also has to know the time in order to know the exact position of the plane throughout the flight. Time is thus the fourth dimension. Time, space, mass, and movement exist in interrelationship with each other, and the greater the density of the mass, the more curved the space surrounding that mass will be. Light emitted from celestial bodies, when passing by huge masses like the sun, will follow a curved line, because in the vicinity of the sun, space is more curved. Light and energy also have masses, because matter and energy are one, according to the famous formula $e=mc2$, in which e is energy, m is mass, and c is the speed of light. The presence of matter brings about the curved nature of space; therefore in relativity, the absolute straight line of Euclidian mathematics is no longer possible.

Chapter Four: Cutting the Net of Birth and Death

1. Alfred Kastler, *Cette étrange matière* (Paris: Stock, 1976).

2. Anuradha Sutta, Samyutta Nikaya SN 22.86; (PTS) S iv 381.

3. J. Robert Oppenheimer, *Science and the Common Understanding* (New York: Simon and Schuster, 1954), p. 40.

4. Literally, "Death, if anyone sees to the depth, is called a hero." See Isshu Miura and Ruth Fuller Sasaki, *The Zen Koan* (New York: Harcourt Brace Jovanovich, 1965).

5. Erwin Schrödinger, *WhatWhat Is Life?: With Mind and Matter and Autobiographical Sketches*, (London: Cambridge University Press, 1967), pp. 138ff.

6. Interestingly, in the latest unification theories, superstrings are supposed to give rise to space and time themselves.

7. Fa Cang, Wang Jin Hai Yuan Guan ("Ending Illusions and Going Back to Your Own Source"), no. 1876, Revised Chinese Tripitaka.

8. David Bohm, *Wholeness and the Implicate Order* (London: Routledge & Kegan Paul, 1980).

Chapter Five: Look Deeply at Your Hand

1. Thich Nhat Hanh, *The Miracle of Mindfulness* (Boston: Beacon Press, 1996). Thich Nhat Hanh, *Breathe, You Are Alive!: Sutra on the Full Awareness of Breathing* (Berkeley, CA: Parallax Press1996, 2008).

2. For commentaries on the Lotus Sutra, see Thich Nhat Hanh, *Peaceful Action, Open Heart: Lessons from the Lotus Sutra* (Berkeley, CA: Parallax Press, 2008).

3. In 2005, the author returned for a three-month visit to Vietnam for the first time after thirty-nine years of exile. He returned two more times, in 2007 and 2008. In 2018 the author returned to stay and is currently living in his "root temple," Tu Hieu Temple in Hue, where he first became a monk.

About Thich Nhat Hanh

Thich Nhat Hanh is one of the most revered and influential teachers in the world today. Born in Vietnam in 1926, he has been a Zen Buddhist monk since the age of sixteen. Over seven decades of teaching, he has published over one hundred titles on meditation, mindfulness, and Engaged Buddhism, as well as poems, children's stories, and commentaries on ancient Buddhist texts. Since his exile from Vietnam in 1966, he has been a pioneer in bringing Buddhism to the West, including founding the Plum Village Tradition of meditation practice, which today has ten monasteries and dozens of practice centers in the United States, Asia, and Europe, as well as over one thousand five hundred local mindfulness practice communities. He has built a thriving community of over seven hundred monks and nuns worldwide, who, together with his tens of thousands of lay students, apply his teachings on mindfulness, peace-making, and community-building in schools, workplaces, prisons, politics, and businesses throughout the world.

Monastics and visitors practice the art of mindful living in the tradition of Thich Nhat Hanh at our mindfulness practice centers around the world. To reach any of these communities, or for information about how individuals, couples, and families can join in a retreat, please contact:

PLUM VILLAGE
33580 Dieulivol, France
plumvillage.org

MAGNOLIA GROVE
MONASTERY
Batesville, MS 38606, USA
magnoliagrovemonastery.org

BLUE CLIFF MONASTERY
Pine Bush, NY 12566, USA
bluecliffmonastery.org

DEER PARK MONASTERY
Escondido, CA 92026, USA
deerparkmonastery.org

EUROPEAN INSTITUTE OF
APPLIED BUDDHISM
D-51545 Waldbröl, Germany
eiab.eu

THAILAND PLUM VILLAGE
Nakhon Ratchasima
30130 Thailand
thaiplumvillage.org

ASIAN INSTITUTE OF
APPLIED BUDDHISM
Lantau Island, Hong Kong
pvfhk.org

LA MAISON DE L'INSPIR
77510 Verdelot, France
maisondelinspir.org

HEALING SPRING MONASTERY
77510 Villeneuve-sur-Bellot, France
healingspringmonastery.org

STREAM ENTERING
MONASTERY
Beaufort, Victoria 3373, Australia
nhapluu.org

The Mindfulness Bell, a journal of the art of mindful living in the tradition of Thich Nhat Hanh, is published three times a year by our community. To subscribe or to see the worldwide directory of Sanghas, or local mindfulness groups, visit **mindfulnessbell.org**.

THICH NHAT HANH FOUNDATION

planting seeds of Compassion

THE THICH NHAT HANH FOUNDATION works to continue the mindful teachings and practice of Zen Master Thich Nhat Hanh, in order to foster peace and transform suffering in all people, animals, plants, and our planet. Through donations to the Foundation, thousands of generous supporters ensure the continuation of Plum Village practice centers and monastics around the world, bring transformative practices to those who otherwise would not be able to access them, support local mindfulness initiatives, and bring humanitarian relief to communities in crisis in Vietnam.

By becoming a supporter, you join many others who want to learn and share these life-changing practices of mindfulness, loving speech, deep listening, and compassion for oneself, each other, and the planet.

For more information on how you can help support mindfulness around the world, or to subscribe to the Foundation's monthly newsletter with teachings, news, and global retreats, visit **tnhf.org**.

PARALLAX PRESS, a nonprofit publisher founded by Zen Master Thich Nhat Hanh, publishes books and media on the art of mindful living and Engaged Buddhism. We are committed to offering teachings that help transform suffering and injustice. Our aspiration is to contribute to collective insight and awakening, bringing about a more joyful, healthy, and compassionate society.

View our entire library at **parallax.org**.